n

Fi   *Bass* is
part o   ES. This
collec   e lives
of loca   careers
– who   :ion and
the wo

BC-3

FROM SLAVE TO WORLD-CLASS HORSEMAN:
Tom Bass

Copyright © 1999 by Acorn Books

Acorn Books
7337 Terrace
Kansas City, MO 64114

Library of Congress Cataloguing-in-Publication Data
J.L. Wilkerson
From Slave to World-Class Horseman: Tom Bass / by
J. L. Wilkerson
Library of Congress Catalog Card Number: 99-073722
Series Title: The Great Heartlanders Series
ISBN 0-9664470-3-4
1. Tom Bass, 1859-1934 - Juvenile literature. 2. Missouri -
Biography - History - Juvenile literature - African American
- Slavery - Horses - Equestrian Sports - Midwest.

10 9 8 7 6 5 4 3 2 1

Dedication

For all the friends and supporters of THE GREAT HEARTLANDERS SERIES who understand the importance of providing children the opportunity to learn about their local heroes.

Acknowledgements

Special thanks to Betty Clippinger for sharing her lifelong enthusiasm for and knowledge of horses.
Betty Dixon and Shirley Rapp for their careful attention to detail.

Book production by Acorn Books, Kansas City, Missouri.

Photo Credits:
Audrain County Historical Society, pages 32, 62, 78, 108, 118, 124 and 128.
United States National Archives and Records Administration, pages 4, 104 and 115.
Illinois Institute of Technology (*The Book of the Fair*, 1893), pages 82, 85 and 87.

Contents

1. Born a Slave..1
2. War and Secret Hideouts............................5
3. A Spring for Rejoicing...............................9
4. Helen MacGregor..13
5. Mr. Potts, the Mule...................................17
6. A Gentleman Rider.....................................21
7. Tom's Schooling..27
8. Mexico, Missouri..33
9. Six Dirty Horses..39
10. Disappointments..43
11. Blazing Black..47
12. The First Horse Show................................55
13. The Tom Bass Bit.......................................59
14. Angie Jewell..63
15. Tom Discovers Columbus.........................67
16. A Champion and a Gentleman..............71
17. Miss Rex Arrives...79
18. The Columbian Exposition......................83
19. A World Celebrity.......................................89
20. Bad News, Good News.............................93
21. A Birth...97
22. A Death...101
23. The One-Sided Deal................................105
24. Selling the Black Filly.............................109
25. Barred in Des Moines, Iowa.................113
26. Belle Beach...119
27. Grief..125
28. Goodbye to Champions.........................129
    Postscript..133
    Glossary..134

1

Born a Slave

The falling snow settled over the cluster of cabins. From dozens of chimneys, curls of smoke drifted skyward, like a forest of pale blue trees. The cabins formed a little village, home to almost 1,000 enslaved Africans on the vast estate of Eli Bass.

It was January 5, 1859, and the Missouri winter pushed through every crack of the Gray family's cabin. Presley Gray stuffed rags between the boards. He and his wife, Eliza, had just become grandparents. Presley was making his little home snug for his daughter, Cornelia, and his infant grandson. Eliza added a log to the fire. She had sent most of her 14 children to neighboring cabins. Cornelia and her baby had finally fallen asleep.

The birth was not easy. Cornelia was only a teenager. The baby's father was the son of Eli Bass.

The son, William, would eventually inherit the Bass estate. But even in those dark days of slavery, William's behavior toward Cornelia was considered very improper.

A few days after the baby's birth, a white woman came to the Gray's cabin. She was Margaret Bass, the wife of Eli and the infant's white grandmother. The mistress of the estate traditionally visited the slave quarters to name a new slave. Even though this tiny baby was Margaret's own flesh and blood, the child was part African. His mother was a slave, so he was a slave.

And although everyone knew William Bass was the baby's father, no one expected that William would treat the boy as if he were his son. In fact, just a few months before the birth, William married a white woman, the daughter of another wealthy Missouri family. The newlyweds lived with the Bass family in the big house on the hill. They were expecting their first baby in a few months.

Margaret looked down at the little boy. She could clearly see his resemblance to her own son, William.

"We'll call him Thomas," Margaret said. She explained that Thomas was a family name. The original Thomas Bass was one of the first generations of the Bass family to emigrate from England to Virginia in the 1700s.

A month after Tom Bass's birth, William rode

into the slave village. He stopped his horse in front of the Gray family cabin.

"Bring out the baby!" he called to Cornelia.

Cornelia appeared at the doorway holding tiny Tom Bass. William lifted the infant onto his horse. No one knows what William Bass said when he first saw his son. The slaves who witnessed the event are long since dead, and they did not record the words of William Bass. His words were unimportant. What was important – and what was passed down from generation to generation from that day onward – was that Tom Bass sat on a horse when he was one month old.

That was indeed important. It was a fitting start for a tiny baby who would become one of the world's greatest horsemen.

$200 Reward.

RANAWAY from the subscriber, on the night of Thursday, the 30th of Sepember,

FIVE NEGRO SLAVES,

To-wit: one Negro man, his wife, and three children.

The man is a black negro, full height, very erect, his face a little thin. He is about forty years of age, and calls himself *Washington Reed*, and is known by the name of Washington. He is probably well dressed, possibly takes with him an ivory headed cane, and is of good address. Several of his teeth are gone.

Mary, his wife, is about thirty years of age, a bright mulatto woman, and quite stout and strong.

The oldest of the children is a boy, of the name of FIELDING, twelve years of age, a dark mulatto, with heavy eyelids. He probably wore a new cloth cap.

MATILDA, the second child, is a girl, six years of age, rather a dark mulatto, but a bright and smart looking child.

MALGOLM, the youngest, is a boy, four years old, a lighter mulatto than the last, and about equally as bright. He probably also wore a cloth cap. If examined, he will be found to have a swelling at the navel.

Washington and Mary have lived at or near St. Louis, with the subscriber, for about 15 years.

It is supposed that they are making their way to Chicago, and that a white man accompanies them, that they will travel chiefly at night, and most probably in a covered wagon.

A reward of $150 will be paid for their apprehension, so that I can get them, if taken within one hundred miles of St. Louis, and $200 if taken beyond that, and secured so that I can get them, and other reasonable additional charges, if delivered to the subscriber, or to THOMAS ALLEN, Esq., at St. Louis, Mo. The above negroes, for the last few years, have been in possession of Thomas Allen, Esq., of St. Louis.

WM. RUSSELL.

ST. LOUIS, Oct. 1, 1847.

Slavery was legal before the Civil War. The St. Louis slave owner who printed this handbill was offering a reward for a family of five runaway slaves. When the Civil War started, one person in 11 was a slave in Missouri. Tom Bass was one of the slaves.

4

2

War and Secret Hideouts

Helen MacGregor slept soundly in her stall. The giant mare was William Bass's champion saddle horse. Tom Bass curled up beside her. He could smell her warm coat, like a blend of cut grass and wood smoke. She snored softly, and a little spot on her withers twitched.

"You dreaming, girl?" Tom whispered. He stroked her long mane. The sleeping horse seemed to recognize his hand, and she leaned into it, as if to say, "Do that again, Tom Bass."

Presley Gray was Eli Bass's coachman. That made it easy for Tom to spend much of his time in the barn. Even as a toddler Tom roamed the stalls, walking under the horses' bellies, patting their legs. When he was four, Tom rode alone on the mare. William let Tom ride her everywhere. People watched in amazement as the tiny boy galloped past.

Tom loved his granddad and grandma. He loved his mother, too, though he hardly ever saw her now that she had been moved up to the big house. But next to his family, Tom loved Helen MacGregor better than anything. He figured she was the best horse in all of Boone County, Missouri, maybe in the whole United States of America.

Unfortunately, people in the United States had little time for fine horses like Helen Mac. It was the Civil War. The country had split in half over the issue of slavery. People in the southern half of the country, the part where most slave owners lived, decided to form their own country. Southerners were fearful that the federal government would soon pass an emancipation law – a law to free the slaves. The southerners called their new country the Confederate States of America.

President Abraham Lincoln said the south didn't have the right to leave the union. When South Carolina Confederate rebels fired on a U.S. military base called Fort Sumter, Lincoln called for Union volunteers to put down the southern uprising. Except for the border states, Missouri, Kentucky, Maryland and Delaware, the other states lined up in support of either the south or the north. And so the Civil War began.

Tom Bass didn't know about any of this, but he'd heard rumblings in the slave quarters – talk about emancipation. Some of the slaves talked about running away, maybe joining the Union

Army. But no one ran away. The Bass estate was in the middle of a large pro-Confederate area. The area was called Little Dixie because so many people from Kentucky, Tennessee and other southern states had settled it.

Helen Mac twitched again, and Tom stroked her neck. "I wouldn't run away without you," Tom said softly.

The barn was dark. The last groomsman had blown out the lantern and pushed the heavy doors shut as he left. This was one of Tom's favorite times. He listened to the soft sounds of the sleeping horses. The smell of leather and hay filled the air.

Right about now Grandma Eliza would be standing at the cabin door and looking out toward the barn. She knew Tom was in there, and though she worried that he spent so much time in the barn, she also knew that her horse-loving grandson was probably safer in the barn than anywhere else in Little Dixie.

Tom had almost fallen asleep when he heard voices. At first he thought it was his grandma coming to get him. But it was white men's voices, and one Tom recognized. William Bass.

"Anybody see you cross the creek?" William was saying.

"No," said the other man. "I stayed in the woods, but I saw those Yankees by the railroad station."

"They'll probably be up here tomorrow," said William, "so we better get you in the house. Keep this rag over that bullet hole, or you'll leave a bloody trail."

Just as William predicted, Union soldiers showed up at the Bass mansion the next day. They searched the house, from attic to cellar. They knocked on wall paneling, listening for any hollow compartments behind the boards. They opened every wardrobe and cabinet. They finally left at sundown without finding the Confederate soldier.

About three hours later the southerner slipped out the back door of the mansion and into the woods, carrying a knapsack full of food. A fresh bandage covered the bullet hole in his shoulder.

Tom Bass could see this from a crack between the boards of the barn. He peered up at the mansion. Just then someone blew out a candle in one of the big rooms upstairs. Tom knew about that room. The Bass estate was a hideout for Confederate sympathizers, including wounded soldiers, running from the Union army. Behind the fireplace was a secret hideout, built by one of the Bass slaves, a master carpenter.

3

A Spring for Rejoicing

One day in April, six-year-old Tom followed his grandparents up to the mansion. When Tom asked why he couldn't go ride Helen MacGregor, Presley said, "Master Eli sent word to come up to the house. Rebels give up. War's over."

Eli and William Bass stood on the mansion's veranda. Slaves fanned out across the huge yard. Some leaned on shovels, some held laundry baskets, some carried dishrags from the kitchen. Eliza crossed her arms the way she did when she was worried.

"This is a dark day," Eli told the crowd of Africans. "We've lost the war."

Like many slave owners, Eli assumed that most slaves happily accepted their servitude. He also believed slaves didn't know what was going on in the world. In truth, for many generations Africans

maintained a news network of friends and family across the country.

William stepped forward because Eli suddenly grew pale, gripping his chest.

In a few weeks, Eli Bass would be dead.

William told the slaves, "The Union government has seen fit to steal from us." He looked at his stricken father and said angrily, "They're taking much of our land – payment for war crimes, they say."

Like other southern sympathizers who helped the Confederates, the Bass family now had to surrender some of their wealth to the federal government.

"We've called you here to say that you're free," said William. "I guess the government means to make you free in every way – 'cause they're not paying us what you cost us and— "

"Free, sir?" Presley interrupted.

"Yes. Free," said William. He went on complaining about the federal government taking "his property." But none of the Africans listened after he said, "Yes. Free."

Free. The word hung in the air like the sweet smell of honeysuckle. Everyone stood motionless, as if the slightest breath could blow it away. Tom remembered that no one slept for days afterwards, letting the full, glorious meaning soak in.

Eli knew most of his former slaves didn't have any place to go now that they were free. He also knew they didn't have money to buy their own farms. So Eli asked if they would be sharecroppers. That meant the freed slaves would farm his property in exchange for part of the crop. Some of the former slaves didn't want to stay on the Bass farm, but some, like Presley Gray and his family, stayed.

Soon after the emancipation announcement, Presley made a decision. He walked up to Eliza who was out on the front stoop trimming Tom's hair. The April sun was shining. Tom could feel the gentle warmth of the sun on his newly exposed scalp.

"Lizzy," said Presley, "I want to get married."

Eliza looked at her husband in astonishment. "What are you talking about?"

"You and me, Lizzy," he said. "I'm talking about *us* getting married."

"We're already married, Presley Gray," she said. "I think this freedom thing has made you addle-brained."

Presley and Eliza had been married for 30 years. Most slave owners didn't let slaves marry. But Eli and Margaret Bass were particularly fond of these two and so the couple was allowed to marry.

"That doesn't count anymore," said Presley. "You and me are free Americans now, and I want us married under the American Constitution."

As a grown man, Tom Bass told this story many times. Young as he was, Tom remembered that spring of 1865. It was fitting that freedom should come in spring. All nature seemed to rejoice in the happy news. The birds sang, and lilacs filled the air with a sweet perfume. The Spring of the Great Emancipation. A new life, full of promise, was beginning.

4

Helen MacGregor

Tom was glad his grandparents remained on the Bass farm. That meant he could stay close to Helen MacGregor. Some days Tom would take off the saddle and bridle, and then the boy and mare would fly across the farm like an exploded cannonball. Even when Tom had to do chores, Helen Mac followed him around like a loyal puppy.

Eliza worried that Helen Mac would accidentally trample Tom. "That big horse could squish him like a bug," she told Presley.

Many times Presley saw Tom whispering to the horse. The horse's head leaned against the boy. They looked like two long-time friends sharing a secret. Few things gave Presley more joy than watching his grandson on the great mare. Tom rode with perfect balance, as if he were attached to the horse.

"Let the boy be," Presley told Eliza. "Our people

13

have lived with fear too long."

William Bass also noticed Tom's exceptional skill. The year after the Civil War ended, William found Tom in the stable, cleaning Helen MacGregor's saddle.

"I'm taking her to the Boone County Fair next weekend," said William. "You'll go along, too." William wanted Tom to do odd jobs around Helen Mac's stall at the show. "Maybe you'll learn a few things about the horse business."

Tom did indeed learn. William eventually took the boy to fairs all over the region. Tom learned the language of horsemen and the rules of competition. Tom listened to trainers talk about rocking-horse canters and longe-line exercises. He heard breeders talk about horse conformation and pedigree.

At the horse show in Boone County, Helen MacGregor lost the champion of show to a stallion named "Charger." Tom was very disappointed. He rode Helen Mac everyday. William was too busy overseeing the farm and seldom rode the mare. If Tom had been the one to show her at the fair, he felt he could have blasted Charger all the way back to Kentucky.

That night Tom shared his frustrations with his grandparents.

Eliza was mending the collar of Presley's white Sunday shirt. "Win or lose," she said to Tom, "a gentleman doesn't make a spectacle of himself."

"The boy didn't make a spectacle," Presley said.

"Did you, Tom?"

"No, sir," said Tom, and then added, "I'm going to ask Mr. William if I can ride Helen Mac at the next show." Tom pointed to Presley's white shirt. "I could wear Granddad's shirt and black boots— "

"That's crazy talk," Eliza said. "Horse shows are for white folks. They'd never let a colored boy – colored man, for that matter – ride in the same ring with a white man."

Tom had never understood why, as a mixed-race person, he was considered all black. It just didn't make sense – "pedigree-wise," he told Eliza. But his grandmother said Tom would never be accepted at a white social event – and horse shows were social events. She'd explained this to Tom a hundred times.

"I don't want to dance with white folks," Tom

said. "I just want to ride horses." All he wanted was to go where the best horses gathered, and that meant going to horse shows. "I ride Helen Mac more than anyone," Tom protested, "that's why I should be the one to show her. I've practiced all the gaits with her. We've even jumped a four-rail fence."

Eliza said, "You might jump over the moon, Tom Bass, but white folks aren't ever gonna let you ride in their horse shows."

"They will if I'm good enough." Tom said it so softly he was sure no one heard him, but when he looked over at his grandfather, Presley winked at him.

A few weeks after the horse show, Tom walked up to the barn. Several men stood at the entrance. One of them was William. Tom wondered if one of the horses had run off. Immediately a sharp pain shot through Tom. What if Helen Mac was gone? He ran to the barn. William held Tom's shoulder as the boy tried to run inside.

"She's dead, boy," William said.

5

Mr. Potts, the Mule

For weeks after Helen MacGregor's death, Tom went about his chores hardly speaking. He wouldn't go near any of the horses. Presley and Eliza worried about him.

One day Presley called Tom to the pasture. He pointed to the Grays' mule, named Mr. Potts, grazing in the distance. "That mule is getting fat," said Presley, "and I got no time to exercise him. I want you to do it."

Tom was about to protest, but Presley stopped him. "'Course Mr. Potts might be more than you can handle. Stubbornest mule in all Missouri."

Of all the things Presley could have said to talk Tom into working with Mr. Potts, that was it: "more than you can handle."

The next day Tom put a saddle and bridle on Mr. Potts. "I'll teach him to round up the milk cows," Tom said. "That should be exercise enough for today."

Presley just grinned and sat down in front of the cabin. If there was one thing that made Mr. Potts extra stubborn it was wearing riding gear. The 15-year-old mule had been known to sit down in the middle of Main Street in Ashland, Missouri, and refuse to move for hours.

Tom mounted Mr. Potts. "Let's go, mule," Tom said.

The boy and mule had barely passed the Gray cabin when Mr. Potts suddenly lowered his back end and sat. Tom toppled off backward and landed in the dusty road.

Presley held back a laugh. He knew first hand the frustration of working with Mr. Potts. That's why the mule had been retired to the pasture for the last five months.

Tom disappeared behind the cabin. In a few minutes he reappeared carrying a long, thick rope. He tied one end of it around the mule's neck.

"If you're figuring to pull him up," said Presley, "I can save you the trouble. Once he gets himself planted like that you might just as soon try yanking an oak tree up by its roots."

Tom was silent. After tying the rope securely around Mr. Potts' neck, Tom ran it along the animal's back. Then he began pushing the rope under the mule's back end. It wasn't easy. Tom had

to rock Mr. Potts back and forth in an effort to force the rope under him.

Even with all the rocking, Mr. Potts didn't pay the slightest attention to Tom. The mule looked straight ahead. His long, jackrabbit ears flitted back and forth, swatting at horseflies.

With the rope at last positioned under Mr. Potts' rump and between his legs, Tom stood beside him. With one end tied around the mule's neck, the rope now ran down its back to his tail, then passed under his rump and finally came out between his legs.

Tom wrapped the loose end of the rope around his hand and gave it a sudden jerk. The rough rope scraped against Mr. Potts' tender backside.

The mule's ears shot up. His big brown eyes looked at Tom.

"You ready yet?" Tom asked.

The mule yawned lazily.

Presley stood up to cheer the boy on. "You've got his attention, Tom," he said. "I do declare you've got his attention now."

Tom hoisted the loose end of the rope over his shoulder. And then, with all his weight, he jumped forward, yanking the rope as he went.

This time Mr. Potts felt the sliding rope burn his tender hide. He honked loudly and shot up. In an instant, Tom leaped onto the saddle. He pulled at the rope again, and Mr. Potts trotted off toward the cow pasture.

Presley laughed and whooped as Tom and the mule disappeared up the road in a cloud of dust. Presley called after them, "You'll have him cantering before you know it."

⤟ 6 ⤠

A Gentleman Rider

A few years after the Civil War, William Bass moved his white family to Columbia, Missouri, where much of his business was now located. The Bass family occasionally returned to the farm so William could meet with Presley and the other sharecroppers.

One Sunday afternoon, William's oldest white son, who was a few months younger than Tom, brought two of his friends to the farm. After lunch the three boys ran off to the corral to ride horses.

Tom was working nearby and heard the boys' laughter. He tiptoed to the corral fence, peering at the boys from the shadow of the barn.

Dressed in fancy riding pants, the white boys mounted the saddle horses and circled the corral, as if performing at a horse show. They yelled commands to the horses and yanked at the reins in an effort to make the animals perform. One boy even used a little riding whip to smack his mount's neck. For all the force and whipping, the horses didn't respond to the confusing commands.

William Bass's white son saw Tom hiding.

"Come here, boy," he yelled.

When Tom turned to leave, the three boys raced through the corral gate and cut him off. His white half-brother, sitting high on a handsome Bass stallion, stood directly in front of Tom.

"I told you to come here," he said. "Don't you know how to behave when a gentleman talks to you?"

One of the other boys stared down at Tom's dusty overalls and bare feet, and said, "Maybe we should teach him some manners."

"Or teach him some riding," said the third boy.

"That's it," said the Bass boy. "I'm going to give you a riding lesson."

At that Tom pushed past the boys and horses and continued down the hill to the cabin.

"Where do you think you're going?" shouted the Bass boy.

"If you're going to teach me riding," Tom said, "I

guess I better get some riding clothes and my saddle horse."

The boys laughed all the way back to the corral. They knew Tom didn't have any riding clothes, much less a horse. No black person on the Bass estate had enough money to own a saddle horse.

⁓

Eliza and Presley were standing just inside the door when Tom entered the cabin. They heard every word from the corral.

Eliza held Tom's head in her calloused hands. "I'll brush off Granddad's white shirt and Sunday coat," she said to him. She knew without asking that Tom was planning to stand up to the bullying boys.

"I'll need his hat, too," said Tom, "and boots."

Eliza nodded. "I'll spit polish 'em."

Presley headed out the door. "I'll saddle up one of the mares," he said.

"No," Tom said, grabbing his grandfather's arm. "I won't ride a Bass horse. Saddle up Mr. Potts. He's ours, and ours is good enough."

"Then I'll brush him till he shines like a brass spittoon," said Presley.

As he hurried off toward the pasture, he was thinking about Tom riding Mr. Potts in front of the white boys. They'd surely laugh. Presley had no

idea why Tom would set himself up for such ridicule – riding an old, broken-down mule into a corral with prized saddle horses.

The white boys had forgotten about Tom Bass, until they saw the bowler-hatted rider coming up the hill.

"We can't teach you to ride like a gentleman if you're riding a mule," said the Bass boy when he recognized Tom.

"A real gentleman can ride anything and look good doing it," said Tom.

"Not a mule," said Bass.

"You look like one of those clowns in a circus," said one of the boys.

All three friends warmed to the idea of watching Tom as if he were a clown in a circus. They dismounted and climbed on the fence.

Tom and Mr. Potts entered the gate and circled the corral slowly. The old mule's clumsy stride made the boys giggle. They pointed at his sagging belly and his drooping lower lip. With his head hung down, the lip almost dragged the ground. Mr. Potts' coat was combed smooth as glass, but he was, after all, a mule.

24

Tom sat erect. He held the reins lightly. He and the mule made one complete circle of the corral.

And then it happened.

The change was gradual. Mr. Potts raised his head. His neck stretched and arched. As mule and rider made their second circle of the corral, Mr. Potts seemed to suck in his big belly, as if he were trying to make himself taller. And indeed, he looked taller to the boys on the fence. They had stopped laughing.

Something strange was occurring. This mule was slowly turning into a horse. By the third circle, Mr. Potts' clumsy stride had lengthened into a smooth glide.

Tom held the reins to one side. Mr. Potts turned and circled in the other direction. His glide turned into a fast-paced prance, each hoof hitting the ground separately in a four-beat gait.

"The mule is racking," said the Bass boy in astonishment.

Slender and tall, Tom rode with the stately ease of a prince riding to his coronation. Even when the mule picked up speed, sailing around the corral, Tom remained poised.

From the corner of his eye, Tom noticed

William Bass standing at the corral fence. His grandparents and other sharecroppers watched, too. Their presence didn't disrupt Tom's concentration. He had practiced these gaits with Mr. Potts for many months in secret. He could have done them in his sleep.

Almost imperceptibly Tom slowed the rack to a canter. Mr. Potts' gnarly front knees, one at a time, snapped up to the mule's chin with the precision of a long-legged show horse. This was one of the hardest gaits for horses.

The boys on the corral fence cheered. The other spectators applauded. No one had ever seen a mule canter. Tom led Mr. Potts to the center of the corral. Facing the spectators, the mule lowered himself onto one knee – a bow to his audience.

Mr. Potts stood again on all fours. Tom tugged gently at the reins, and the mule moved backwards. His walk quickly picked up speed and in a few moments he was cantering backwards. No one in Missouri had ever taught a mule – or a horse either – to canter backwards.

Eliza held her hand over her mouth. She didn't know whether she was stopping herself from laughing or crying. She just didn't want to make a sound that would break the concentration of the mule. With her other hand she held onto Presley's arm. Presley patted her hand.

"The boy's a natural," he whispered.

7

Tom's Schooling

In 1870, Presley and Eliza left the Bass farm. They bought a little house in Columbia, Missouri. Tom helped them load their belongings and harness Mr. Potts to the wagon.

Just before Presley climbed onto the wagon seat, he turned to his grandson. "I'm wanting to talk a moment about your schooling, Tom."

Lately Tom's education was his grandfather's favorite subject. When Presley was Eli Bass's slave, no one noticed that the quiet coachman always listened intently to every business deal discussed within his presence. He studied every deed and book left unattended. In a time when teaching an African to read and write was a crime, Presley had taught himself both.

But Tom had never been interested in going to school. He'd only completed third grade. Working with horses took all his time.

"Every day I'm learning about the horse business," said Tom. "I don't need all that book stuff, reading and `rithmatic and such."

"Horse business is white man's business," said Presley. "And a white man knows about reading and `rithmatic. He knows all those fine, fancy words in legal documents, and he knows how to count out money and to see to it that he gets the correct change. You don't know any of it, and you're aiming to get yourself cheated in a white man's business."

"I'll think about it," Tom said.

This was the way the school conversation usually ended – Tom saying he'd "think" about going to school. But Presley wanted his talented grandson to set his sights on more than being a stable boy for the rest of his life.

Presley was a proud man. He'd already told Eliza that now that they were leaving the farm he would never again wear overalls. He bought Eliza a big bolt of white cloth and told her to make him several shirts.

"That's what I'm wearing from here on out – white shirts and Sunday pants," said Presley. Presley Gray lived for almost 30 more years, and true to his word, he never again wore overalls. Even when digging in his city garden, he put on a white shirt and string tie.

"My sharecropping days are over," he said.

Tom didn't go back to school. He stayed on the farm and worked for William. His father bought and sold horses at the Columbia auction house.

"I'll buy some renegades," said William one day. "Nobody wants them 'cause they're ruined – trained wrong or beaten up. But I guess a fellow who can make a mule canter can make a renegade behave."

"I can't *make* a mule – or horse – do anything," Tom said. "But I can teach them to *want* to."

Tom knew that William could buy renegades cheaply. After Tom had taught them to trust hu-

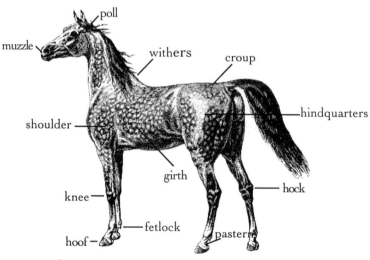

The parts of a horse are called "points." These are some of a horse's points.

29

mans, William then could resell them for a big profit.

The first renegade William bought was a stallion. Four men struggled to push the raging animal into its stall. When Tom looked over the stall door, a pair of wild eyes looked back at him. The stallion was as tall as Helen MacGregor, but he was much thinner. Tom opened the gate.

"Don't go in there, Tom!" William shouted. "At least take a pitchfork or whip. I've seen him trample a man."

"Looks like someone's already whipped him," Tom said angrily when he saw the thick welts across the animal's withers.

The tall stallion spun around until he faced Tom. Tom lowered his head. He didn't want to make direct eye contact with the horse. That posture was confrontational. It meant, "I want to fight you."

Tom stepped into the stall. The horse stamped his feet and tossed his head furiously. It was a clear warning – Keep Away! Tom took another step – not directly at the horse, but toward him – all the time talking softly. He dangled his hand a few inches from the muzzle. The stallion snorted.

"No more whips," Tom whispered.

The stallion lifted his long, handsome head toward Tom's hand. The soft lip brushed against Tom's fingers. As gentle as a feather, Tom stroked the muzzle. Then Tom quietly turned and walked out of the stall.

"That stallion's a killer," William said, as they left the barn. "Why'd you take a chance like that? Don't you realize he could kill you?"

Tom just smiled. "If he'd wanted to kill me, he would have told me."

Tom is standing behind two unidentified women. The only clue to the identity of one of them is a note on the back: "Tom, with Mother."

8

Mexico, Missouri

Tom looked up at the sign: Ringo Hotel. A bearded man stood in the hotel doorway calling orders to someone behind the front desk.

"Are you Mr. Louis Hord?" Tom asked.

Hearing his name, Hord turned to the young man standing in the street. Nineteen-year-old Tom was covered in road dust. For three days he'd hiked and hitched rides until he arrived in Mexico, Missouri, a town considered by many westerners to be the center of horse breeding and training.

"I'm Tom Bass," he said, and handed Hord a piece of paper. It was a note from Joseph Potts, a man Tom met three years earlier at the Boone County Fair. Along with his partner, Cyrus Clark, Potts owned the Mexico Horse Sales Company, one of the biggest horse businesses in Missouri.

Hord read the note and said, "Potts says you're looking for work."

"Yes, sir," Tom said. He'd kept Potts' note behind a photograph of his grandparents. Every week Tom took the note out, looked at it and put it back. Maybe he was better off staying on the Bass farm. Tom remembered Presley's warning – being cheated in a white man's business. But he also thought about all those fancy horses up in Mexico. On a spring day in 1878, Tom pulled the note out again. By now the paper was worn as thin as a horsefly's wing. But this time Tom didn't put it back behind the photograph. This time he slipped it inside his suitcase.

"What sorta thing you do?" Hord asked.

"Horses," Tom said.

Hord's face brightened. He said he needed someone that very minute to drive the hotel's carriage to the train station to pick up guests. Starting that day, Tom became the hotel's driver and soon afterwards the head of the Ringo Hotel stables. Before long guests and townspeople were bringing Tom their horses, especially the troublemakers.

One person in particular noticed Tom's work at the Ringo Hotel: Joseph Potts. His growing company sold saddle and harness horses to people all over the country. The operation required a large crew – smart people who knew how to find good horses and train them. Potts wanted to hire Tom.

Cyrus Clark, Potts' partner, said no. It wasn't that the Mexico Horse Sales Company didn't have blacks working for it. It did. Black people worked at horse farms and horse companies all over the country. They cleaned stalls, polished equipment, and combed horses. Some black people even exercised the horses.

Potts, however, was suggesting that Tom buy and train horses for the company's annual sale. Every year before the big sale, the crew scoured the countryside for good horses. All of them carried company money. After paying for the horses, the crew brought the animals back to Mexico to prepare them for sale. Each crewman was in charge of cleaning and training his own string of horses.

Training could take several months. On the day of the sale, each trainer worked as the handler for his horses, displaying the animals to potential buyers.

Tom had plenty of experience preparing horses for sale, but he'd never done any of the rest of it. Potts knew that Tom was good enough for the job. Clark said that wasn't the point.

"He'll be representing the company in front of our customers," Clark protested. Like many prejudiced people, Clark seemed to be implying that other people's racial attitudes – not his own – made Tom a poor candidate for the job. "White people aren't going to want to do business with a black man. And what do you suppose our crew will think when we bring in a former slave to work shoulder to shoulder with them?"

"We'll take it one step at a time," said Potts.

Clark wouldn't budge. "You want to risk it, fine. Let him use your money – not the company's – to buy horses."

Potts grinned. "That's a deal, as long as I get any profit his horses make at the sale. My investment, my profit. Agreed?"

Clark agreed. He didn't even expect to see Tom return to Mexico after he pocketed Potts' money, and certainly not return with saleable horses.

Shortly after Tom was hired the situation at the company became desperate. With only two months before the annual sale, Potts and Clark called a staff meeting. Dozens of horses had to be found and trained.

Tom sat in the back at the meeting. He raised his hand, as if he were in a schoolroom. Tom said he knew about a few good horses down in Boone County, his old home territory.

Clark didn't say anything. But when Potts pulled out a wad of ten-dollar bills, Clark rolled his eyes heavenward. "That's the last you'll see of your money," his look seemed to say.

Potts ignored his partner. He handed Tom the big roll of dollars.

"Bring me some good ones, Tom" he said.

Tom lived most of his life in central Missouri. He worked for a short time in Kansas City, Missouri. The Bass estate, where he was born, was located near Ashland, Missouri, 16 miles south of Columbia.

9

Six Dirty Horses

Four days later, Tom rode up to the company barn. Six horses followed behind, tied together in a long line, nose to tail. When Clark and Potts came out for a closer look, even Potts was disappointed. Underneath the thick coat of road dust, the horses were as plain as any family's ordinary buggy animals. Their coats were full of brambles and their feet were unshod.

Clark looked at the bill-of-sale for the six horses. "At least they're cheap," he said to Potts.

Other crew members brought in their newly purchased horses. Soon the company barn teemed with animals and people. Getting ready for the big sale required a thousand daily chores. Raking out stalls, bringing in hay, re-shoeing, fitting bits, exercising horses, etc. Tom helped, like the other crew members. At every free moment, he doted over his six horses. He made sure they had extra helpings of molasses and that their stalls had an extra layer of straw.

With the sale two weeks away, Potts and Clark held another meeting. The sale catalog needed to go to the printer. Every horse had to be listed – its name, pedigree, age, special features, any limitations. Like any good company, Potts and Clark guaranteed the quality of their horses.

At the meeting, Potts and Clark called the name of each crew member. One at a time the men brought their horses into the auction ring and announced the information about the animals.

Tom listened for his name.

Finally Potts called, "Tom Bass."

Word had spread that Tom's horses were the dregs of the sale, but everyone had been so busy getting ready that no one paid much attention as Tom prepared his horses.

Tom led three of his inexpensive farm horses to the center of the ring.

"Whose horses you got there, Tom?" someone asked from the sidelines.

The animals following Tom were silky and smooth. Tom lined them up ten feet apart, leaving each one standing alone, its lead rope hanging to the ground. The beautiful horses stood perfectly still, as if Tom had formed them from wet, red clay.

"What did you do with your horses?" Clark asked. "And where'd you find these?"

"They were renegades I worked with a few years ago," Tom answered. "I trained them lady-safe. Everybody favors a gentle horse. The other three are back in the stalls. I'll go get them, if you like, 'cause they're just as sweet as these."

Potts lit a cigar and grinned broadly. "That won't be necessary," he said, and turned to his partner, who shook his head in bewilderment. "Will it, Cyrus?"

Potts made a handsome profit on the six horses. Because of his deal with Potts, Clark didn't make any money on Tom's string. But he never made the same mistake again. From that day on, Clark never doubted Tom's abilities. Many years later he told a friend, "Tom Bass is the best judge of horses I have ever known."

41

10

Disappointments

As soon as the 1879 horse sale ended Tom and the others began looking for animals for the next sale. That summer, while riding by a farm north of town, Tom spotted a beautiful black mare. She stood alone in the pasture. The other horses stayed in a back corner, as if keeping their distance from the mare.

Tom found the farmer harvesting hay across the road and asked him how much he wanted for the horse.

"Most anything you're willing to give," said the farmer. "She's crazy. Meanest animal I ever saw."

Tom hadn't seen any horse this beautiful since Helen MacGregor. "Mean" and "crazy" were meaningless terms to describe a horse, as far as Tom was concerned. Tom struck a deal with the farmer and that afternoon he headed off toward Mexico, Missouri, with the black mare tied to his buggy.

43

Potts and Clark came out of their offices when Tom rode in with the mare. Stable boys and trainers drifted outside to see her, too. She was indeed a beauty.

Seeing the men, the big mare reared, and Tom's buggy jerked backward. The mare kicked her back legs at the approaching crowd. She was spooked and determined to let no one come near her.

And nobody did. They'd all seen horses like this — eyes filled with anger; teeth snapping; sleek legs thrashing, powerful enough to crack a skull or crush a ribcage. In the horse trading business they were called "spoiled," meaning worthless.

Tom assured everyone that the mare was just a little nervous coming into a town. "She'll get used to it," Tom said.

But when it took five men to put her in the stall, no one believed him.

For the next few weeks, Tom visited her every day. On his first visit, he merely stepped through the stall door and waited until the mare stopped snapping and stamping. When she finally calmed down, Tom left. Later when he opened the stall door, the mare was quiet until Tom took a step toward her. Again he waited until she had settled down, and he left. Each time he returned to the stall he moved a little closer to her.

And always he talked to her. His soft, calming voice never let up. Potts said it sounded as if Tom were singing her a lullaby. Tom asked how she liked her grain, if the straw bedding was soft enough, what size bit she'd like to wear.

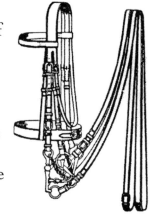

Tom finally put a saddle on her and a few days later he rode her around the corral. Though she was the most beautiful horse in the stable, Potts and Clark decided she required too much time to train and so they sent her to pasture. She'd make a good broodmare, they decided.

On the day the black mare went to pasture, Potts passed her empty stall and saw Tom inside holding her bridle. He looked so forlorn that Potts patted him on the shoulder.

"Can't win 'em all," he told Tom.

Tom's life centered on horses. He trained and rode horses during the day. He talked with his friends about horses during meals. Sometimes he stayed up all night with a sick animal.

Tom hadn't gone to school as his grandfather hoped. He did go to church, however. Tom even learned to read the hymnal when he found out that the girls often shared their hymnals with boys sitting next to them – *if* the boys could read the words.

Tom's church attendance increased after the black mare went to pasture. The church's social life helped take his mind off the horse's forced retirement.

At the Mexico church, one girl in particular liked sharing her hymnal with Tom. Her name was Mimi Johnson. On summer evenings, Tom took Mimi on long, romantic buggy rides around Little Dixie. He told her about the trips he'd made to far-off places like St. Louis and Kansas City with William. He told her about the wild horses he'd trained. Before long, Tom charmed the sweet-natured Mimi.

Several months after the black mare went to pasture, Mimi became pregnant. She gave birth to twin boys, named Ray and Ralph. They were Tom's sons. In a few years Tom would become famous, and therefore much is known about his public life. But no one knows why he and Mimi never married. She and Tom's twin sons lived most of their lives in Mexico, Missouri, but Tom wasn't part of their lives. This was sad and puzzling, especially since Tom knew better than most people the hurt and loneliness that comes from not having a father's love and attention.

Tom loved horses. Maybe he loved horses too much. Sadly, his devotion to horses would cause more sorrow in the years to come.

11

Blazing Black

Joseph Potts sat with his feet perched on top of the desk. He blew a cloud of cigar smoke toward his toes.

"What we need's a top-class mare," he said to the crew gathered in his office.

With the next sale only weeks away, the company needed a "brag" horse, an animal with obvious championship potential. The company owned a champion stallion, Thornton Star. But Star was old, his show days coming to a close. Some of the most influential horsemen in the U.S. and Canada planned to attend the company's sale, and these people expected to see superior animals.

Clark said mournfully, "I don't know a horse in all of Little Dixie that can hold a candle to some of those Bluegrass mares. And even if we find one, there's no time to train her."

Tom leaned against a back wall. He'd been with

the company for two years. "We've already got a show mare," he said.

"Where?" Clark asked, as if he knew there was no such mare.

"Up in the pasture," Tom said.

Potts sighed. "He's talking about that spoiled black horse."

"She's a champion," said Tom. "You all come out tomorrow morning, bright and early, and see for yourselves."

No one in the room was willing to wager that Tom wasn't telling the truth. They knew Tom too well for that.

The sun barely glimmered along the eastern horizon. Its pale light sparkled through the trees. Pinpoints of dew clung to the tips of leaves and then dropped silently into the tall, wet grass.

Tom stopped his horse and buggy beside the pasture. A little stream ran under the road and meandered into the field, finally spreading out into a large shallow pond.

A blue mist rose up from the water. It settled over the ground, reminding Tom of the steam that rises up from a team of horses riding hard on a winter day. Clusters of horses – chestnuts, bays, roans, grays, blacks, duns – stood in the mist, like painted creatures in a fairytale.

The black mare stood alone in the misty water. She leaned down to get a drink. Tom opened the gate and whistled, two quick notes, like the sound of a bob-white. The mare instantly lifted her head.

The two walked toward each other. As Tom neared her, the mare bared her teeth threateningly.

"Mind your manners," he said, as he fitted her with the halter. He led her to the buggy and pulled a currycomb from his grooming box. He combed the dark coat. Before long the mud and cockleburs were combed and brushed away. The black mare shone like polished ebony.

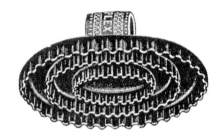

"Now don't you feel better?" Tom asked.

Tom lifted the saddle from the buggy and just as he cinched it in place a wagon came down the road. Potts, Clark and several others had decided to accept Tom's early morning invitation.

As soon as the mare saw the wagon, she stamped the ground aggressively. She tried to pull away from Tom, but he held firm.

"I see she's still a sweet, little kitten," one of the men called out. Everyone in the wagon laughed.

Tom tipped his hat and smiled at the joke. He

49

rarely tried to talk someone into his point of view. Tom wasn't a talker. He had learned that doing mattered more than talking.

Tom mounted the black mare. When she felt the slight pressure from Tom's knee, she turned and walked down the road away from the wagon. With the men out of her view, the mare began to relax. Tom signaled for her to turn again. This time she stood facing the wagonload of men who sat watching the magnificent horse many yards away.

Clark stood when the mare turned to face the men. "Lordy, she's a beauty," he said. Even from that distance he could see her great eyes, so wide they looked like white beacons in her black face.

Another signal from Tom sent the mare cantering toward the wagon. In perfect timing she loped toward the men as if she were floating. Her long black neck arched liked a bow. When she passed the wagon, she snorted. Her hooves hit the road in the three-beat rhythm of the gait, with a heavy accent on the third beat. One, two, three. Ba-Da-Boom. With each step, little clouds of fine dirt swirled around her feet.

Several yards beyond the wagon, the mare turned again. With hardly a pause, she charged toward the men in a rack — the high-stepping gallop of a saddle horse. The rhythm changed to four beats. One, two, three, four. Pow-pow-pow-pow. The sound echoed over the pasture like a drum roll.

By now everyone in the wagon was standing. As they watched her perform each gait, Potts and Clark realized they had a new dilemma. The problem wasn't finding a brag horse for the company. They obviously had a champion mare. The problem was who would show her. She was more than headstrong. She was a firebrand. The only person who could ride her was Tom Bass.

Tom rode the mare to the wagon. Despite the cool morning, her coat was covered in sweat. She bared her teeth at the men and lowered her ears.

"She's a winner," said Clark, "but who's going to ride her in the Mexico horse show next month?"

Tom didn't say anything, and he made a point of not looking directly

51

at his other boss. With his ever-present cigar, Potts
was staring at Tom. The two had become friends
during the last two years, sometimes talking late
into the night about the horse business and about
Tom's future. Potts encouraged Tom to save his
money and open up his own stables someday. Without looking at Potts, Tom knew what his boss was
thinking. Potts always spoke his mind, loudly and
passionately.

"Tom's the only one can ride her," Potts said.

"That's what I mean," said Clark. "Tom's the
only one can handle her, so how're we going to
show her?" Everyone knew what he meant: the
mare had the skill to perform in a major show; only
Tom had the skill to ride her; Tom was a black man;
black men didn't ride in horse shows – ever.

Tom rubbed a large towel over the mare, wiping
away the sweat. He knew Clark and Potts had their
backs against the wall. Tom had found them a
champion mare and had trained her to obey the
classic saddle horse commands. He had done his
job. The rest was in their hands.

"I don't know if I have to paint you a picture,
Cyrus," said Potts. "What I'm telling you is Tom's
going to ride this black mare in the show – pure and
simple."

Cyrus Clark was a businessman. If he'd thought
he would lose money by letting a "colored boy," as
he called Tom, ride a company horse in a show then
Clark would not have allowed it.

Tom held his breath. Long ago he had learned to hide his feelings, to conceal his hurt from a father who never treated him as a son, to mask his frustration at hearing other riders receive applause on horses he'd trained. Potts had just spoken the words he had dreamed of hearing all his life: Tom Bass will ride in a horse show.

"I guess the horse world better get ready," Clark said. He nodded toward the mare, and then toward Tom. "Because we've got a couple of surprises for them."

Tom ducked his head as he rubbed the mare. Tears welled up in his eyes, but he brushed them away on his shirtsleeve so fast that no one noticed. Years later he would confess that this was the one time he nearly cried in public.

All Tom ever wanted was to train and ride horses. Riding in a horse show was just the next logical step in the life he had chosen. With all his hopes and expectations, Tom never once set out with a goal to change history. But he was about to do just that. Within a few weeks his life would change forever – the world of horse showing would change forever – when Tom Bass, a former slave, rode into a show ring on a horse, aptly named Blazing Black.

⟾ 12 ⟾

The First Horse Show

Sweat beaded up on Tom's forehead, causing his hat to slide forward over his eyes. He gripped the reins so hard that his nails dug through his riding gloves. As he waited in the parade line to enter the ring, the nervous tension made him feel sick. Tom wasn't the least bit afraid of Blazing Black, even though she'd started her usual teeth-baring at everyone.

What knotted up his insides was all those people in the bleachers. Hundreds of Missourians, Kentuckians and other important people in the horse business sat in the arena at the Mexico Horse Show. Presley, too, was in the audience.

Just before Blazing Black stepped into the ring, she backed up and reared her head. Rather than adding to Tom's nervousness, this merely calmed him. Tom might have flinched from hundreds of spectators staring at him, but Tom Bass knew horses.

Tom pressed his legs into her sides, and the mare instantly moved forward. His gentle body commands, which riders called aids, were as familiar to her as a halter and saddle. Circling the ring in the opening parade, Blazing Black settled into the familiar rhythm of the gaits. Like any great athlete, her instincts and the months of hard training took over.

Tom's fears, however, returned. When he and Blazing Black re-entered the ring for the mare-class competition, Tom was so tense he could hardly breathe. He held the reins too tightly. He sat too rigidly. Before long Blazing Black was confused. When the judges called for the trotting horses to "Rack on!," she tried to respond to the rhythm changes of the other horses. But without Tom's familiar aids, she hesitated.

At one point, Blazing Black was supposed to pivot. When she turned, Tom looked up in the audience. Clark sat with his head downcast. Beside him, Potts stood. Holding his cigar daintily, as if handling a teacup, Potts bobbed his hand up and down. He seemed to be begging Tom to lighten up on the reins. All of this only made Tom more nervous.

Further into the pivot, Tom spotted his grandfather. The old man sat erect. His white shirt was so

bright it seemed to
light up his
bleacher section.
There was some-
thing about that
white shirt...It
seemed to say,
"I'm a free man.
I'm your equal."

From head to
toe, Tom felt his
rigid muscles loosen. Fear and doubt lifted. Blazing
Black sensed the change. Her whole body seemed
to rise up into the saddle as she felt Tom gain his
composure. Through the rest of the show, Tom and
the black mare sailed through the required gaits.

Potts danced a little jig in the aisle. Even the
calm Clark raised his hands overhead and clapped.

Ba-Da-Boom went the canter. Pow-pow-pow-
pow went the rack. The audience applauded loudly.

The judges called out the three top horses. Blazing Black, "with Tom Bass up," was called. She won
second place, the red ribbon. Potts and Clark were
angry at the decision. Tom was not.

Tom broke every racial barrier at his first horse
show. But no one protested or caused trouble –
although in the future this would not always be the
case. Tom had turned a terrible early-show performance into a spectacular late-show performance.

That great performance would become the standard that other riders would have to reach for the rest of the horse show season.

As far as Tom was concerned, he was a winner.

13

The Tom Bass Bit

During his first show season, Tom rode every show horse the company owned, including Thornton Star. Like all good riders, Tom attracted the attention of the town's young boys, black and white, who wanted to work with horses.

One of those boys was Potts' nephew. A most amazing thing had happened: Tom had taught the nephew to ride Blazing Black, even to perform with the horse during recent shows.

"What's the trick?" Potts asked Tom. Nobody had ever mounted the black mare except Tom. "Did you hypnotize the boy – or the mare?"

Tom laughed. He told Potts he'd be back in a few minutes, and then he left. A little while later he returned. He laid a strange horse bit on Potts' desk.

"That's the trick," said Tom. "Blazing Black's been wearing that bit for almost a year."

Tom told Potts that he'd designed the bit in such a way that it wouldn't hurt the horse's mouth. Bad-fitting bits often tore up a horse's tender gums.

Tom never whipped a horse. In a time when clubbing an animal into submission was common practice, Tom's endless patience and his way of talking to horses was considered odd, even if successful. Now he had invented a bit that greatly reduced the chances of damaging a horse's mouth.

"This'll make you a rich man, Tom," Potts said. "But you've got to get it patented."

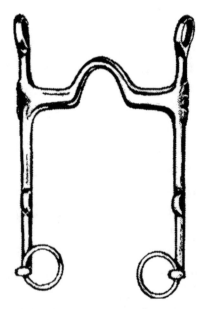

Especially useful when training a horse, Tom's bit was lighter in weight and less chafing to an animal's gums than other bits.

"I don't want all that paperwork, filling out forms and keeping track of government papers," said Tom. "That's fine for you and Mr. Clark. I just want to make these bits and see to it that horses I work with wear them. I'll give them to anyone who'll put them in a horse's mouth."

"But you could sell them, Tom, make a fortune," said Potts.

"I'll sell them for what it costs to make them. I'm not after getting into the bit business," Tom said firmly.

For better or worse, Tom stuck to his decision. Potts helped Tom get money from the bank to start manufacturing the bits – but only after Potts assured him that nobody except Tom had the right to change the design of the bit.

Before long the Tom Bass Bit was used throughout the horse world. Invented by a former slave more than one hundred years ago, the bit has never been off the market. Its inventor never made a dime from its sale. He told Potts the bit was his gift to horses.

After Angie Jewel, a schoolteacher, married Tom, she helped with his new horse business. She oversaw the business correspondence, financial management and bookkeeping.

14

Angie Jewell

Around the time he designed the Tom Bass Bit, Tom met a young woman named Angie Jewell. Angie, who taught at the school for black children, had recently moved to Mexico, Missouri, with her little sister.

Angie liked Tom. His handsome looks, quiet charm and well-known talent with horses appealed to her. Of course, all these things appealed to many young women in Mexico. In fact Tom's reputation as a "heartbreaker" was well established.

Tom borrowed a fancy buggy from Joseph Potts for his first date with Angie. But when he came to pick her up, he was surprised to see Angie and her sister standing arm-in-arm at the front door. Angie explained that the little girl would accompany them.

Seeing Tom's disappointed, Angie said, "A chaperone will do wonders for your reputation." She pointed out that he was a respected horseman. "A man of your position," she said, "should have a chaperone when he escorts a young woman."

Finally, after a long and thoroughly chaperoned courtship, Tom and Angie married on September 20, 1882.

⁓

The next year Potts and Clark sold their business. Tom didn't want to go to work for another company. Now that he had a wife, Tom especially wanted to establish his own roots – both with a business and a home.

Potts said he'd help. "I'll go with you to the bank," he told Tom. Potts said he'd guarantee a loan to buy land.

Tom picked out four acres just north of Mexico, and Potts' lawyer drew up the papers. Before long Tom was standing on his own property. He and Angie looked around at the tall grass, wild raspberry bushes and a thicket of hickory trees. If he'd had a hammer and wooden planks Tom would have started on the barn and house that very day. But first he had to get the money.

On one of his many horse-hunting trips around the region, Tom bought a one-eyed colt. With its long pedigree, the little horse was far too valuable to live a life pulling a milk wagon or other drudgery work, the fate of most damaged horses. After proper training, the injured colt would bring a good profit. That money would help finance Tom and Angie's house and barn.

The day before Tom sold the colt he pulled a little leather bag from his pocket. Tom always carried the little bag, which was filled with kernels of corn. Angie figured the corn was treats for the horses, and yet she'd never seen Tom offer them to a horse. One day she asked him about the little bag.

"It's for counting," he answered sheepishly. Tom confessed that he couldn't do the arithmetic needed to buy and sell horses – at least he couldn't do it on paper.

But Tom had a method. For example, when the farmer with the one-eyed colt asked a certain price for the animal, Tom told the farmer he would think about it. Even if Tom were willing to give the amount the owner asked, Tom always left the deal unfinished. In private he would pour out the kernels of corn from the bag. Each kernel stood for each dollar Tom had with him. From that pile of kernels he would then take away the number of kernels that the horse cost. The remaining kernels represented the amount Tom had left after the transaction.

For anyone who knew arithmetic and how to handle money, Tom's method was complicated and slow.

Angie shook her head in disbelief. She knew Tom struggled with reading and writing. Even before their wedding, she had tutored him. Two or three nights a week she pulled him away from the barn for his lessons. He read aloud and practiced writing.

"Don't horse sellers ever wonder why you can't make a decision on the spot?" asked Angie.

Tom shrugged his shoulders. "Maybe they just think I'm real cautious."

He told her that one time he had to come all the way back home before he could make the deal. A horse owner had seen the little bag of corn and asked if he could feed some to his horse. Tom couldn't say no. What reason could he give for denying the man's horse a few kernels? So Tom stood by and watched as the horse ate his arithmetic system.

Tom never told anyone about his system. He was too ashamed.

Angie rummaged through the textbooks she had used as a teacher. She found a math book and laid it on the table. She could see that Tom was embarrassed.

"We're going to have you adding, subtracting, multiplying and dividing before the weekend," she said brightly and sat down beside him. "You've already mastered the hard part – knowing horses like the back of your hand. Math's the easy part."

⊹— 15 —⊹

Tom Discovers Columbus

One spring day Tom passed a herd of grazing cows. In the same pasture was a lone colt. The little white gelding darted through the herd, stopping occasionally to see if one of the calves was following. The colt clearly wanted to play.

Playfulness wasn't unusual for a colt. What was unusual was its speed. Tom had never seen a horse that young move so fast.

By then Tom knew arithmetic. When the farmer said he wanted one hundred dollars for the colt, Tom counted out 10 ten-dollar bills.

Shortly before sundown Tom rode up to his barn with the colt tied to the buggy. Angie came out to look. For almost six years, she and Tom had talked about finding a "brag" horse, one that could compete with the fine horses at other stables.

The colt buried his muzzle in Angie's apron. He could smell the good cooking from the kitchen. Angie immediately loved the new horse.

Tom said that all the way home he'd thought about a name for the white colt and decided to call him "Columbus."

"Columbus discovered America," said Tom. "And I discovered Columbus."

Columbus would become the first champion horse owned, raised and trained by the Bass stables. Perhaps Columbus knew his glorious future because from his first day at his new home the little colt established himself as prince of the barn.

The day's work at the barn always started early.

Tom was in the stalls by 5:30 a.m. to feed his horses. But with Columbus' arrival the schedule changed. The little gelding wanted his breakfast at five – no later. He whinnied loudly until Tom showed up with his meal. When Tom didn't appear with food at the right time, Columbus created such a commotion that the other horses in the barn also began neighing and stamping.

"Who's training who?" Tom asked as he poured grain into the little horse's stall.

When he wasn't being trained, Columbus followed Tom. Tom soon learned that, like the white gelding's food schedule, Columbus was determined to have his way about being with his human family.

One day Tom had to go to town, so he put Columbus in the corral and fastened the gate. Tom had almost reached the town square when a shopkeeper pointed down the street.

"Someone's on your trail, Tom Bass," he said.

Tom looked back and saw Columbus. The gelding had used his teeth to unlatch the corral gate. Not even ropes tied around the gate kept Columbus corralled. If he couldn't open the gate, he crawled under the fence rail. When Tom blocked that exit, Columbus jumped the fence.

Columbus also liked to visit Angie. One day she found him standing in the middle of her kitchen. He'd opened the door and come in for the cookies she left in the window to cool. Angie discovered that Columbus also liked pies. Although Angie was very fond of Columbus, she learned to keep her doors locked.

16

A Champion and a Gentleman

Shortly after Columbus came to the Bass barn, Tom received terrible news. Grandmother Eliza had died.

Eliza and Presley lived in what was known as the "colored section" of Columbia, Missouri. When Tom arrived, horses and buggies lined the street near their house. Presley stood in the front parlor next to the opened casket. He was dressed in a black suit with his usual white shirt. When he saw Tom, he nodded to his grandson to come in.

"Don't let in the flies," he said to him.

Lying on a lacy pillow, Eliza wore a flowered dress and satin shoes. She was so tiny that it was hard for Tom to imagine she'd spent most of her life at the hard labors of slavery.

Tom and Angie stayed for the wake on the first

day and the funeral on the second. The house was full of friends and neighbors. Even William Bass, Tom's father, stopped by. The two had long since grown apart.

As during other times in his life when sadness or worry pressed in on him, Tom turned his attention to horses, keeping busy to ease his grief.

Forty horses – some owned by Tom, some by other horsemen – lived in his barn. Every day was spent feeding, grooming and training them.

All Tom's spare time, however, went to Columbus. The gelding grew into a giant white horse. After almost two years of training, he was ready for competition. At the start of their careers, show horses usually competed in small events. But Columbus was a fast learner, so Tom decided to enter the gelding in the St. Louis Horse Show, one of the biggest events in the country.

Tom had competed in hundreds of shows by the time he and Columbus walked into the St. Louis ring. He'd won dozens of prizes. But on that day Tom was the first black man to ride in the St. Louis Horse Show.

Local newspapers reported the entrance of Tom and Columbus in the opening parade. It was breathtaking – a tall, regal black man on a giant, white gelding.

Columbus' long neck arched proudly. His white coat was brushed to a sheen. Tom was dressed in high, black boots, hat and a riding coat with brass buttons.

For months before the St. Louis competition,

Tom and Columbus practiced the complicated routines for a special kind of event called "high school." This show event was very popular at the time. A high school horse performed fancy footwork – two-legged turns and impressive leaps. A high schooler danced. While the band played, the horse stepped to the rhythm of the music. Judges ranked the horse and rider on the originality and difficulty of their routines.

Unlike the five-gait competitions, high schoolers came into the ring one at a time. The judges studied every movement as the rider and horse performed.

Columbus pranced through his routine as if he'd danced in the St. Louis arena every day of his life.

The performance was so close to perfection that some of the other riders, watching in the wings, applauded. A group of horse people from Mexico, Missouri, including Joseph Potts, watched, too.

When the high school event ended, the judges called for "Columbus with Thomas Bass up" to re-enter the ring. They had won the competition.

All that night and the next day, crowds of people who had seen the remarkable performance came to the show stables to meet Tom and Columbus. Potts watched as his former employee received a stream of congratulations.

Suddenly someone in the crowd yelled, "What's your real name, boy?"

Everyone in the stables was quiet. For the most part, the fact that Tom was a black man had not caused trouble at the St. Louis show. When he first entered the ring, a few hecklers booed, but they were soon quieted by the performance of Tom and Columbus.

The angry man in the stables stood in front of Tom. "What gives you the right to call yourself the same name as the man who invented the Tom Bass Bit?"

Years later people who knew Tom Bass were asked to describe him. The one word they repeatedly used was "gentleman." It was not his nature to raise his voice or his hand against either a human or a horse. Confronted by the bigot, Tom thought of his grandmother who had once told him that a gentleman doesn't make a spectacle of himself. And now Tom knew why. A gentleman doesn't have to. Tom was a champion horseman. His winning performance in the ring represented a lifetime of hard work. He had proven himself in front of his professional peers. Who needed a spectacle after that?

To the man standing before him, Tom said simply, "I *am* Tom Bass."

"You mean you took your slavemaster's name?" the man asked, still refusing to believe that a former slave could have invented something as important and widely used as the Tom Bass Bit.

A bigot was dangerous. Anger against a black person sometimes turned into violence. Lynchings were common in the region, especially in Little Dixie. Less than a year earlier, a relative of Tom's had spent the night with Tom and Angie. He was running from a gang called the "White Caps," who accused him of stealing a white man's hunting dog. They planned to hang him. Lynchings were a constant nightmare for black people. In the 1890s more than 1,000 lynchings occurred in the United States.

Fearing a fight, many in the crowd backed away. Only Joseph Potts stepped forward.

"You're talking to the gentleman who invented that bit," he said to the man. "And he's the only Tom Bass I've ever heard tell of."

Tom's cool demeanor and Potts' firm support silenced the racist. He left without another word.

Although Tom never faced a lynch mob like his relative, he encountered racism many times in his life. The incident in St. Louis wouldn't be the last – or the worst.

In the next few years Columbus and Tom won ribbons and trophies all over the country. Tom taught Columbus to canter backwards, and the gelding became the first horse in history to perform that feat in competition.

Columbus eventually attracted the attention of the nation's most famous showman: Buffalo Bill Cody. When the famous creator of the Wild West Show asked to buy Columbus, the blood drained from Tom's face. Of course he couldn't sell him. The fantastic giant gelding was his first brag horse and the showpiece of the Bass company.

But Tom realized that all horses were for sale in a horseman's barn. The sale of horses kept the business operating. Tom had several other horses and foals at the time. These, too, would be trained

 as saddle horses. He couldn't, he told himself, become too attached to one horse.

Buffalo Bill offered to pay a handsome price for Columbus. Unfortunately he was in financial difficulty at the time and couldn't pay for Columbus right then, but he promised to come back for the horse.

Meantime, Tom and Columbus continued to compete together in shows across the country. Sometimes when they returned home to Mexico, the townspeople gathered on the square and clapped as Tom rode the great gelding from the train station to the Bass stables. He and Columbus performed for the crowd, ending with Columbus rearing up on his back legs as if to salute the audience. Later in the Wild West Show Columbus was the star attraction for children. No other horse Tom owned was as popular with the public as Columbus.

For many years Columbus continued to give Tom great joy. Pain and tragedy also were ahead. And there would come a time when that beautiful white gelding would break Tom's heart.

Columbus with Tom Bass up.

17

Miss Rex Arrives

One day a Mexico breeder, Ben Glenn, asked Tom to come by his farm. Glenn had a new foal, the offspring of his best broodmare and another owner's champion stallion named Rex Denmark.

When Tom arrived at the Glenn stables he found a skinny, gray filly lying in the straw. Still wet and shaking from its sudden arrival in the world, the baby hardly looked like a future champion. But Tom knew what to look for, that's why Glenn had asked Tom to come.

Tom knelt beside the tiny foal.

"I'm naming her 'Miss Rex'," said Glenn.

"That's a good name," said Tom, examining the filly, "because she's as fine as her daddy. Look at these eyes – big and bright and far apart. High withers. Long back." Tom ran his fingertip along the base of one of the little ears. "Well-rooted ears," he said.

Best of all were her long, slender neck and face. These and other characteristics in the filly and other carefully bred horses eventually led to the development of the American Saddlebred. Tom helped establish this distinguished type of horse, which became an official breed three years later in 1891.

"I'll have to sell her," said Glenn. "If she's as good as you say, I've not got the time or money to spend on her."

Glenn said maybe he'd ask $300 for her, which was $100 more than he usually asked. Tom knew he couldn't afford to pay what she was worth, but he told Glenn that Joe Potts would buy the filly.

"You think $300 is too much, Tom?" Glenn asked.

"It's not enough," Tom said. "I'll tell Mr. Potts that he'll have to pay $350 for her."

Tom was frank with Potts. He told him Glenn would sell the filly for $300, even less if Tom advised it. Potts had thought about buying a champion mare from Kentucky named Lou Chief – already a powerhouse of a horse that had the whole horse world abuzz – and he was about to send Tom to the Bluegrass state to buy her. But Potts trusted Tom's opinion about Glenn's filly. Tom said Miss Rex was champion stock and well worth the money and that's all Potts needed to know.

"I'll buy her, Tom," Potts said, "on one condition – you train her."

Tom was honest with both Glenn and Potts. Both men gained. Tom gained nothing – except the chance to train and ride a horse that eventually became one of the most famous saddle horses in the world.

The Columbian Exposition was the 1893 World's Fair. It was held in Chicago, Illinois, and all the buildings, streets, waterworks, statues and parks were built especially for the event. The six-month fair included more than 65,000 exhibits. At that time about 63 million people lived in the United States – 27 million tickets to the Exposition were sold! More people attended the Columbian Exposition than had ever attended any event in the history of the world. The grand buildings of "The White City" became the inspiration for the architecture of American public buildings for the next 40 years.

18

The Columbian Exposition

In 1892 a group of businessmen from Kansas City, Missouri, visited the Bass stables. Tom was often in Kansas City on business trips and knew most of the men. They were members of the Commercial Club, later called the Chamber of Commerce. They came to Mexico to talk Tom into moving to Kansas City. They wanted him to open a livery stable there.

For several decades Kansas City was the last outpost on the western frontier. The town was known for its gamblers and gunslingers, and for its ankle-deep muddy streets.

The Commercial Club wanted to make Kansas City respectable. The town was already a railroad hub, with nearly two dozen rail lines. But in those days, any respectable city needed a first-class stable, operated by an expert horseman. Would

Tom come to Kansas City and open such a business?

Neither Tom nor Angie wanted to leave Mexico. Their family and friends lived in the area. But the Kansas City job was a once-in-a-lifetime opportunity to expand the Bass horse business. So Tom and Angie decided to live in the big city for a few years, save their money and return to Mexico. Tom would keep a staff in Mexico to run the stable there.

Soon after Tom moved to Kansas City, a letter arrived inviting him to the World's Fair in Chicago.

Held in 1893, the fair was called the Columbian Exposition, in honor of the 400th anniversary of Christopher Columbus' arrival in North America. Actually Columbus arrived in 1492, but the exposition was so large that it took an extra year to organize.

Tom's invitation to perform was a great honor. At the Exposition's Horse Show, the Champion of the World would be crowned. Tom decided to take Miss Rex, now five years old.

The night before his first competition, Tom walked to the fair's amusement park. Near its center was the world's first Ferris Wheel. As the giant wheel spun slowly, the passengers in the swaying chairs laughed and screamed. Some gripped the

The world's first Ferris Wheel, 264-feet tall, was at the 1893 Columbian Exposition.

safety bars as if fearful that the whole contraption might fall apart.

Tom watched the wheel's grinding engine. Whether it was a Ferris Wheel or a locomotive, the world was set in motion more and more with engines. Tom was glad. He wanted someone to build a wagon with an engine, a buggy with an engine – a saddle with an engine! When fellow horsemen heard Tom say this, they couldn't believe their ears.

"Do you want the horse to disappear?" they asked.

Tom said the horse would never disappear. He

said that the Emancipation Proclamation had made him a free man, and that the engine would be the emancipation of the horse. No more back-breaking work pulling heavy wagons. No more dangerous work carrying soldiers into battle.

"People who love horses will go on riding them," he said, "because there is nothing like riding a fine horse."

On the first day of the competition, Tom waited in the huge hallway behind the bleachers. Miss Rex's big brown eyes looked around at the other horses. Nothing else about her moved. She might have been one of the marble statues along the Exposition's avenues. Her competitors tossed their heads and whinnied nervously. A dainty gray lady, Miss Rex was smaller than the other saddle horses. Maybe too small and maybe too easy-going for a show horse, some people said.

In the years to come, Miss Rex would amass unbroken records of victories. Presidents and Queens would know her name. In her lifetime, the most famous and victorious horse from Missouri was a stallion named Rex McDonald. The only horse ever to beat him was Miss Rex. But on that day in Chicago only a few people had heard of her. Within two hours that would change.

Tom heard his name announced. He signaled to Miss Rex to move to the entrance of the arena. Only a few feet ahead of them was the opening to the show ring and 10,000 spectators.

As Miss Rex lifted her leg into the ring an amazing transformation occurred. Suddenly the little mare from Missouri turned into a silver butterfly. She arched her neck and lowered her face until it was perpendicular to the floor. And then she drifted across the ring as if she'd grown wings.

Tom had taught her well. Miss Rex moved flawlessly through the five gaits. She glided from walk

This is the inside of the Transportation building at the 1893 Columbian Exposition. The latest in buggies and other transportation equipment were on display.

to running walk to trot to canter to rack and a half dozen variations as smoothly as cream pours from a pitcher. She cantered diagonally. She spun in circles. She skipped. And when it was over and the audience stood to applaud, Miss Rex faced the judges. She was frozen in place, not a hair twitched, while Tom lowered his head in a formal bow.

Many of the best saddle horses in the world appeared in Chicago that year. The judges had to pick one as the First World Champion of the Columbian Exposition. They picked Miss Rex.

19

A World Celebrity

Telegraph wires buzzed with the news of Tom and Miss Rex's victory. Hundreds of people in Chicago stopped by to see the celebrities. People from France, Germany and Austria, who barely spoke English, wanted to shake Tom's hand.

President Grover Cleveland went to the Exposition barn to visit the champions. After his second election, Cleveland asked Tom to ride in his inauguration parade. Tom and Cleveland remained friends, writing each other letters until Cleveland's death in 1908. In the years to come, Presidents William McKinley, Theodore Roosevelt, and William Taft visited Tom in Mexico, and he twice performed before President Calvin Coolidge.

Back home, Tom's stables became a tourist attraction. Visitors wanted to see Miss Rex, the Champion of the World, and meet the man who trained her.

One man particularly was interested in the champion. He came all the way from Europe. His name was Mr. Fleming, and he represented Queen Victoria of Great Britain. Fleming wanted to buy Miss Rex and take her back to England to the Queen's stables.

By that time Miss Rex was owned by one of the richest men in the United States, Mr. S. H. Fulton, a railroad owner. Like Potts, he bought Miss Rex only under the condition that Tom continue training her.

Fleming wrote Fulton a letter. Queen Victoria would pay $6,000 for Miss Rex. When Fulton refused the offer, Fleming persisted. Fulton, however, said the champion mare wasn't for sale – at any price.

Finally Fleming gave up. But he returned to Missouri to make a special request. Would Tom bring Miss Rex to Great Britain and perform at Queen Victoria's Diamond Jubilee? Scheduled for 1897, the jubilee celebrated 60 years of Victoria's reign.

Fulton and Tom talked about the invitation. Travel expenses and lodging would be paid. Angie could go, too. For several days, Angie planned and dreamed of the trip. She couldn't understand why Tom waited so long to accept the Queen's invitation. Finally Tom admitted that he couldn't make the trip. He didn't want to go on a ship.

"I don't want to be out of sight of a tree," he said.

Tom had ridden some of the wildest horses in the country. He had performed dangerous exercises on a horse – in a few years he would nearly die while performing high school. He was a very brave man. Nevertheless, Tom was afraid of traveling on boats.

No one lost respect for Tom because he wouldn't go to England. In fact, some people came by his stables expressly to meet the man who had said no

to the Queen. Tourists still came to his barn. Horsemen still sought his advice. His reputation as a world-class horseman grew daily.

But Tom's life was far from trouble-free. The rich society people who valued his advice and bought horses from him made Tom go to the back door when he came to their houses. When he and white riders went to horse shows, Tom's friends stayed at hotels, while Tom slept in the stalls with the horses. The audiences who applauded him at the horse shows, later dined at the white-only restaurants, while Tom cooked his supper on a camp stove.

Tom was an expert whose opinion was highly valued by everyone, including presidents and royalty. But he was sometimes treated as if he were less than the animals he loved. Angie confided to friends that this treatment ate at Tom's spirit, often making him depressed.

⧼═20═⧽

Bad News, Good News

A fter Eliza's death, Presley visited her grave in the segregated cemetery every day. When the old man became too frail to walk, Tom left money and instructions at a local livery stable for a carriage service.

Presley lived to see his grandson dazzle the world with his horsemanship. When Presley was too feeble to travel to Tom's horse shows, Angie sent him newspaper clippings. Tom gave his grandfather many of his trophies and ribbons.

Soon after the end of the 1896 horse show season, Presley died. He was 84 years old. When Tom heard the news, he ordered a white silk shirt from Kansas City. He bought a solid walnut coffin, the finest he could find in Columbia. Tom could imagine his grandfather smiling at the fancy casket and clothes. Presley had spent 55 of his 84 years in slavery, but the old man would be buried in style.

Returning home from the funeral, Tom talked to Angie about his grandparents. He told her about Eliza worrying when he rode Helen MacGregor, and about Presley cleaning up Old Potts on the day the mule cantered backwards. Angie listened quietly. As they rode into Mexico, Angie said that she and Tom would make good parents, too, like Eliza and Presley.

When Tom gave her a puzzled look, Angie said, "You and I are going to have a baby." After 15 years of marriage this was a big surprise.

The day after Angie told him the news, Tom bought a two-wheel basket cart and a black and white pony. Now Tom would have someone he could teach everything he knew about horses, someone who would share his love for horses.

In 1897 Tom received invitations to appear at all the major horse shows, including Madison Square Garden in New York City. But Tom was turning down everything that required him to travel more than a day's journey away. By then he and Angie had moved back to Mexico, and he wanted to be home for the birth of the baby.

Angie looked at the Madison Square Garden invitation. No black man had ever been invited to the Garden.

"I don't think you should say no to this one," she said.

Tom remembered a New Yorker named Alfred Vanderbilt. He was a powerful industrialist who knew about Tom's work in Kansas City. Tom served on the Kansas City fire department's advisory board.

In those days, cities took pride in the horses used to pull fire-fighting pumpers. Highly trained teams of giant draft horses competed at international shows called the Congress of Firefighters. Kansas City leaders wanted to buy German draft horses so their town could compete, too. The German horses were extremely expensive, and so Tom organized a fund-raising horse show. The event was so popular that the city continued the tradition, and a few years later it became the American Royal Livestock and Horse Show. At the first show, Tom performed on Miss Rex and Columbus.

Alfred Vanderbilt had seen Tom at the Kansas City Horse Show. Consequently, the Vanderbilt family insisted that Tom Bass receive an invitation to Madison Square Garden.

With Angie's encouragement, Tom went to New

York and took Miss Rex. If any racists sat in the audience that day, they were silenced by Tom's support from the Vanderbilts. Theodore Roosevelt, who also had met Tom in Kansas City and continued to correspond with the horseman, came by the Garden to see his friend, too.

When Miss Rex and Tom returned home with ribbons won at the Garden, Fulton, the mare's owner, and Tom discussed the mare's future. Miss Rex was almost ten years old by then. Besides the five-gaits, Miss Rex performed high school events, which were extremely difficult and dangerous for older horses. Maybe Miss Rex should retire. As a broodmare, she might produce wonderful champion foals.

"They'll make you a lot of money," said Fulton.

Tom was confused. How could her foals make Tom money? Fulton owned Miss Rex, so her foals would belong to him.

Fulton could see Tom's confusion.

"I'm giving her to you," Fulton said. "You helped her come into this world. You trained and rode her. She's your horse, Tom – she always was."

21

A Birth

Though Tom was happy about Fulton's gift, nothing could compare to his happiness at the birth of his son. On August 10, 1897, Inman Bass was born. Friends from all over the country sent congratulations to the new parents.

Within a few days, Tom carried his son into the stables and introduced him to the horses. Everyone commented about how much Inman resembled his father.

The world of horses and horsemanship filled every room of the Bass home. Trophies and silver platters lined the shelves of a massive display case in the living room. By the time Inman was one year old he had met dozens of celebrities and famous horsemen.

One day William Jennings Bryan, one of the country's most popular politicians, stopped to see

Tom. The big man with the booming voice held the baby up to one of the shining trophies. Inman's face reflected in the polished silver.

"See that face?" he said to Inman. "That is the face of a champion. You have a brilliant future ahead of you."

Despite the pretty ponies – Tom bought his son several through the years – Inman didn't seem interested in horses. The Bass stables attracted every boy in Mexico. They were always hanging around the corral, listening to every word Tom said, trying to learn from the great master. Inman was different. He was more interested in shooting marbles with friends or listening to music on the family's Victrola.

Tom's business depended on his attending horse shows around the country. Shows advertised the quality horses available at the Bass stables. He hated to miss so much of Inman's childhood. When he wasn't traveling, Tom took his son on long horse rides around Mexico. Tom wanted to share with his son the great joy of riding a fine horse.

Despite Angie's careful bookkeeping, Tom was never a good manager of money. His growing family, however, inspired him to build a nest egg. After Inman's birth, Tom sent a letter to Buffalo Bill Cody, asking if the showman was ready to buy the white gelding, Columbus. Cody immediately sent the money and the 10-year-old horse was shipped to the Wild West Show.

As Tom watched Columbus being loaded into the rail car, his only comfort was knowing he could show the white gelding from time to time. That was the agreement struck between Tom and Buffalo Bill.

In 1901, Tom and Columbus performed at the Mexico Horse Show and Fair. At their final presentation, Tom gave Columbus the command to stand on his back legs. The white horse raised himself perpendicular – a spectacular sight because Columbus was a giant horse. Suddenly Columbus toppled backwards and landed on Tom.

Within a few seconds Columbus bounded upright. Tom didn't. The hundreds of people who witnessed the terrible accident believed Tom was dead. Columbus hovered over the limp body, nudging Tom, trying to make his rider wake up.

Tom's pelvis was damaged. Doctors didn't believe he would ride again. He remained in the hospital for several weeks. Telegrams arrived from all over the world. Angie finally had to have the phone disconnected because it wouldn't stop ringing.

Tom could remember only one thing about the accident.

"I opened my eyes and saw Columbus staring down at me," Tom said. "No human has looked at me with more concern than he had in his eyes that day."

It took a year for Tom to recover. But for the rest of his life, Tom's injuries caused him pain. He also lost some of the grip in one of his hands. These were serious handicaps for a horseman who communicated to his horse through gentle movements of his body and hands.

22

A Death

One day Tom returned from a long road trip to a competition in Montreal, Quebec, Canada. Canadians loved Tom. They called him the father of the American horse show and "the greatest living competitor" in the horse-show ring.

When Tom stepped from the train his back ached from the long ride. He looked forward to the warm compresses that Angie would put on his tired muscles.

Tom was helping to unload the horses from the train when he heard the familiar voice of his son.

"Look at me, Dad," Inman said.

Tom could hardly believe his eyes. Inman was riding a bicycle. The boy rode in a circle and then in a figure eight. Tom didn't say a word. He'd seen bicycles in every big city he visited. They were the biggest fad in the country.

That afternoon when Tom walked into the kitchen, he plopped into a chair and sighed. Angie put her arm around his shoulders. While in Kansas City, Tom had organized the Tom Bass Riding Club for boys and girls. The popular clubs had spread throughout the country, and yet Tom's own son didn't like to ride a horse.

"Inman could ride some of the finest saddle horses in the world," said Tom, motioning toward his stables where the great Saddlebreds lived. "Why would he ride some metal contraption that looks like the inside of a clock?"

"Because he's just a boy, Tom," Angie said, trying to comfort him. Inman was 13 years old. At that age, Tom Bass had already trained a mule to canter backwards and had devoted his life to horses.

That year brought Tom much greater sadness than Inman riding a bicycle. News came that Columbus, the beautiful white gelding, had burned to death in a barn fire in Augusta, Georgia.

One night, many years earlier, Tom helped put out a barn fire in Mexico. Above the roaring inferno, Tom heard the screaming horses trapped inside, and later he smelled the stench of their charred remains. He never forgot that sound and smell. Most stable owners covered their stalls with straw or wood chips. But after that night, Tom always used a fine black compost, delivered weekly by a local farmer. Straw and chips were highly combustible. The compost wasn't.

Tom's grief over Columbus worried Angie. She found him late at night in the barn and couldn't get him to leave. Tom remembered the Mexico barn fire – the horror of the flames. The image of Columbus burning alive haunted Tom.

"I can see his eyes, Angie," he said, holding his sides, as if he might be sick. "I can feel his terror."

Nothing could replace Columbus, the horse that helped launch Tom Bass's horse business. But Tom was about to meet another horse – the greatest of his life and the one that would make him smile again.

Tom Bass attended horse shows all over the U.S. and Canada, similar to this one held in Kansas City in 1905. Tom helped organize the original Kansas City horse show in 1894, which eventually became the American Royal Livestock and Horse Show.

⟡ 23 ⟡

The One-Sided Deal

Tom was a great judge of horses – even unborn horses. He loved to match a great stallion with a great mare in hopes of producing an even greater foal. For several years Tom hoped that a famous Missouri stallion named Forest King would be mated to a broodmare named Belle Morris. Tom's old boss, Cyrus Clark, owned Belle.

"A King foal out of Belle will make a mighty fine horse," said Tom.

Clark watched Tom's eyes light up at the thought of the match.

"Could be," Clark said, as if only a little interested. Actually he was hoping to mate Forest King with his broodmare. "Maybe we'll do that someday."

"Why not this spring?" asked Tom.

"Stud fee for Forest King is expensive," said

Clark, a shrewd businessman. He trusted Tom's opinion and believed the foal would be very valuable some day. But Clark knew why Tom was so anxious to arrange the match. Forest King would soon leave Missouri because a Colorado man had recently bought him. "But if you want to pay the fee," Clark added, "I'll gladly give my permission. Of course, I'll own the foal, you understand."

Tom understood. But he didn't know if Angie would. She knew that stud fees were paid by mare owners, especially when owners expected to keep the baby. Tom would gain nothing from Clark's offer – except the joy of seeing a great foal born into the world.

That night Tom brought home a bouquet of

flowers and handed them to Angie.

"What's the occasion?" she asked.

"Belle Morris is going to be bred to Forest King," said Tom.

"What made old Clark change his mind?" she asked. "For years, he's said he wouldn't pay for the match."

"Well, he's not actually paying," Tom said sheepishly. "I am."

"And who'll own the foal?" Angie asked, although she was afraid she knew the answer. Tom just hung his head.

Angie was so angry that her hands shook. She laid the flowers on the table. She didn't speak because she was afraid she'd say something she'd regret.

"I believe this foal will be the greatest of all," Tom said, pleading with his wife to understand why he had made such a one-sided deal. "Trust me, Angie."

For years she had tried to manage the household and business finances. Tom made a good living, but it was almost impossible to make ends meet. He always spent too much money on the horses and charged too little for his services. Forty excellent and expensive saddle horses lived in the Bass barn. "What did he want with one more?" Angie asked herself.

Tom's friends felt the same way as Angie. They couldn't understand why he would pay a stud fee and then let the mare's owner keep the foal. But Tom just closed his mind to their criticisms. Someday he would own that foal. It might take many years, but the foal would be his. Cyrus Clark was a shrewd man. Tom Bass was a patient man. In the end, he hoped patience would win.

Tom Bass is riding Jack O Diamonds, one of hundreds of horses he trained at his stables in Mexico and Kansas City, Missouri. Some of the horses in Tom's stables belonged to him, but some were owned by other people who hired Tom to train their animals. Tom charged about $30 a month to board a horse. Training sometimes took 10 months.

Selling the Black Filly

That spring Belle Morris gave birth to a filly. Tom raced to the Clark barn. Like Miss Rex, the baby was a long-legged, long-necked beauty. But unlike the great silver mare, this little horse was pitch black, except for two white stockings.

Though only a few hours old, she bounced around her mother like a black moth. The filly's spirit and her conformation – the shape and size of her body – were everything Tom had imagined. Given the right training, she could indeed be a champion.

"She's for sale," said Clark. When Tom didn't respond, Clark added, "I figure she'll bring $500."

"I'm sure she's worth it," Tom said.

Tom visited the Clark farm many times during the next few months. At one point, he made Clark an offer – a few hundred dollars for the filly. Clark laughed and said he'd already invested that much in feed and registration fees.

"I'm asking $800 for her now," Clark said.

Tom didn't make another offer, but he continued to visit the foal. Finally after a year, Clark decided to give the filly to his son, Charles. Clark figured Tom would give in and buy the animal when he watched the young boy trying to handle the pretty horse. But Tom didn't yield. When he saw Charles working with the spirited filly, Tom offered to help.

"We can give her a few longe-line lessons," said Tom. Charles, who admired the great horseman, was thrilled for the chance to work side by side with him.

Many years later, Charles Clark remembered those days. He said, "Tom never worked his horses

until they were tired. He made their training work-
outs just like play, so that they wanted to do their
daily routines just as a puppy loved to play with its
master."

For almost three years Tom dropped by the
Clark farm to help train the filly. She grew tall and
regal. Tom knew that a horse needed continual
training in order to become a champion. For a long
time she was too hot-headed for Charles to ride.
Despite Tom's skillful training, the filly hated prac-
ticing the slow gaits. She loved galloping, however,
and was a flash of lightning on the training track.
Crowds gathered to watch her because she could
rack faster than any horse in Mexico.

One day Clark came outside to the track where
Tom and Charles worked with the black filly.

"I've sold her," said Clark. For almost four years
she'd received the best training money could buy,
and it hadn't cost Clark a penny. But he'd grown
tired of waiting for Tom to buy the filly. "Captain
Short from Fort Leavenworth is buying her for his
wife." The captain had paid Clark a large sum for
the horse. "Sure surprised me," Clark said, "but he
just showed up today unannounced – as if he knew
about the filly. Anyway, he's taking her back to
Kansas tomorrow. Too bad you didn't get your
horse, Tom, but it's not like I didn't give you the
chance."

Captain Short's sudden appearance in Mexico,

Missouri, might have surprised Clark, but it didn't surprise Tom. Tom knew the Captain from his Kansas City days. Through the years, the army officer had bought several horses for his wife. Mrs. Short loved beautiful horses and took care of them, but she liked to have a new horse almost every year.

"My wife changes her horses like some people change their hats," Captain Short told Tom.

On Tom's last business trip to Kansas City, he learned that Mrs. Short was looking for a new horse. Tom recommended the black filly at Clark's stables in Mexico. Tom figured Mrs. Short would tire of the little horse in a year or so. The horse would benefit from the light harness work of pulling the woman's buggy. In the meantime, the patient Tom would wait.

25

Barred in Des Moines, Iowa

When Inman misbehaved at home or caused
trouble in school, Tom told him he was
acting like a renegade stallion. This made Inman
mad. "I'm not a horse," he told his father. "Don't
you ever think about anything but horses?" That
was just the way Tom talked – the language used by
people whose lives were dedicated to horses. Tom
didn't know how to be any different.

Tom didn't share everything about his horse
business with Inman or Angie. Some things were
too embarrassing and painful. Perhaps Tom's worst
experience as a horseman was in Des Moines,
Iowa. He had performed at the Iowa State Fair for
many years. But one year as he unloaded the last of
the 16 horses he planned to exhibit, a group of men
stepped forward and blocked his path.

"You're Tom Bass, right?" asked one of the men.

It was a silly question. Everyone in the country who knew anything about horses could recognize Tom. At that time he was at the height of his career. Tom recognized the men. They were the Board of Directors of the fair.

"Yes, sir," said Tom, in his usual polite way.

"A complaint has been registered," said the man. He spoke very formally, as if he were reading from a law book. "One of the fair's contestants says he is uncomfortable riding in the same ring with a colored man. So we must ask you to vacate the premises, Tom Bass."

This had never happened to Tom. He showed horses all across the country, from New York to California. People running shows in Kentucky, Tennessee and Missouri had never barred him, though those states had harsh segregation laws.

In those days, the laws didn't protect people from such injustices. Nothing Tom could do or say would change the board's decision. Tom didn't even try. But when he felt his shoulders start to sag from the meanness and sadness of the situation, he forced himself erect.

Other Missouri horsemen were unloading their horses, too. When they heard the man tell Tom to leave, they gathered around the board members.

"You Iowans afraid of a little competition?" asked Luther "Splint" Barnett. A fine rider, Splint was usually one of Tom's biggest competitors. But he and the others were also Tom's friends. "Maybe *all* us Missourians ought to pack up and leave – give you folks a fighting chance," Splint added jokingly.

"Go if you want," said the man, as he and the other board members turned to leave, "but there'll be no coloreds showing here."

The Missourians didn't leave. Splint had a better idea. Even though Tom couldn't go into the ring himself, his horses could. And so Tom's friends showed his horses, all 16 of them. They won ribbons and prize money for Tom.

But even that victory couldn't erase the pain Tom felt. He didn't tell his family what had happened, but Angie and Inman already knew. Within days the entire country had heard the news. Newspapers from New York to Los Angeles told the story. The *London Times* in Great Britain telegraphed Mexico, Missouri's newspaper for information about the shocking news.

William Jennings Bryan stopped by

William Jennings Bryan

115

Mexico to give his friend support.

"I won't go back to Iowa next year," Tom told Bryan.

"But you must," said Bryan. He shook his fist dramatically. "Rise up like a phoenix, Tom, and sweep through their show until they beg for mercy."

Tom did return to Des Moines the next year. A group of representatives from the fair met Tom when he arrived and told him they regretted what had happened the year before. Everyone tried to make him feel welcome. The bad publicity from the incident had embarrassed the town.

Tom and his horses had a great show. The victories included: first for four-year-old-and-older geldings; champion of the show for harness and saddle classes; first for high school class; first for three-year-old stallions; first in aged stallions; first in three-year-old stallions, combined harness and saddle class; first in yearling halter class. Tom was particularly proud when Miss Rex's daughter, Frances McDonald, won the three-year-old mare class.

And all those prizes didn't even include the

many other red and yellow ribbons. No other competitor in the history of the Iowa State Fair had won so many events in one year.

There was only one event Tom couldn't enter at the Iowa Fair: the American Cup event, which was for Iowans only. A man named Ralph C. Hamilton owned the winning horse.

When reporters asked Hamilton where he found such a great saddle horse, he said, "I bought him from Tom Bass last year."

Tom Bass, world-champion horseman.

26

Belle Beach

The black filly didn't stay in Fort Leavenworth very long. Within a few months, Captain Short showed up at the Bass stables with the horse.

"She pulls a buggy better than any horse I've ever known," said the captain.

"So what's the trouble?" Tom asked.

"She's perfect – until another horse tries to pass her – and then she takes off like a race horse."

The commandant of Fort Leavenworth had issued strict orders that no horse, harness or mount, could go faster than a walk. Speeding horses threatened pedestrians at the fort. In a few weeks, the feisty horse from Missouri had wrecked two light runabouts, a two-seater and a surrey.

Three days earlier, Captain Short's wife had taken the black mare down Fort Leavenworth's main avenue. When a white stallion, mounted by an

army major, pulled alongside her, the filly bolted forward in a breathtaking rack. Horses and people leaped to get out of the way. Luckily, Mrs. Short and bystanders escaped unharmed, but the buggy crashed through a store window.

"The trainer at the fort says he can whip her into obedience," said the Captain, "but Mrs. Short and I don't want her spirit broken." He looked up at the beautiful black horse standing beside him. "Will you buy her, Tom? She's not any good in harness, so I know I can't get much. But I want her owned by someone who'll let her be herself."

And so it was that Tom Bass came to own the horse he had always wanted. Her name was Belle Beach, believed by many people to be the greatest show mare in American history.

Tom was certainly glad to "let her be herself," if only he could figure out what she wanted to be. Belle Beach wasn't nearly as easy-going as the gentle Miss Rex, who would do five gaits all afternoon if she thought it would please Tom. Trying to please was not a concern of Belle.

Gaiting required high-stepping movements. Horses doing five gaits looked like drum majorettes leading a big brass band. Tom thought that maybe Belle Beach was a dancer instead of a marcher. And so he taught Belle Beach some of the fancy and difficult high school routines. The transformation in the mare was immediate. Belle Beach was bigger than Miss Rex and as strong as Columbus. Her muscular body was amazingly coordinated. Her sense of balance was so good Tom joked that she could perch atop a fence rail.

Belle Beach was nervous at her first show. She wasn't used to the noise and the crowd. When the other show horses moved close, her big eyes flashed and she snorted a warning – Back Off! And she still hated for any horse to move in front of her.

When she entered the arena, Belle circled the ring in a canter. Tom then had her do two fast, tight whirls, ending abruptly in statuesque stillness. That was the cue for the band to play a waltz.

At the first musical note, Belle slowly raised her front legs until they reached high above her head. She then turned on her back legs, pivoting in a full circle. This was the high school maneuver that had

121

sent the giant Columbus backward on top of Tom. The sure-footed Belle Beach didn't waver. Still in time with the lilting waltz, she slowly lowered her legs to the ground.

That day, Belle Beach danced to "The Blue Danube" and "Turkey in the Straw." She trotted backwards. And when it was all over, she fell to her knees in a bow to the audience.

Tom later wrote, "I knew then that Belle Beach was an incredible mare. She was a professional, even in her first show."

Few people had trained as many fine saddle and harness horses as Tom Bass. Some of those horses still lived at the Bass stables, but many more lived in stables throughout the U.S. and Canada. Tom was now 50 years old. Belle Beach would be his last great horse. He would say many times that no two horses were alike. But his heart was big enough to love them all. As a boy, he had loved the giant, sweet-natured Helen MacGregor. He had loved the powerful, clever Columbus. He had loved the calm, dainty Miss Rex. Now he was equally devoted to the graceful, fiery Belle Beach.

Tom and Belle Beach performed together for more than 20 years. Belle became one of the most popular show horses in the country. Europeans came to America expressly to see Belle perform.

In 1918 a group of French breeders came to New York to learn about the American Saddle

Horse. They particularly wanted to watch Tom and Belle perform. When they found out that the Madison Square Garden horse show was a month after their scheduled departure date, they extended their stay in order to meet Tom. They later told reporters that Belle's performance was "marvelously impossible." Another European, Queen Marie of Rumania, also admired Tom. She clapped loudly when she saw Tom and Belle Beach in St. Louis.

Tom and Belle danced together. Rather than riding in the saddle, Tom sometimes stood beside the black mare, and they would dance in unison. The fast-stepping Belle had a keen ear for the rhythm of the music. If Tom didn't keep up, she would step on his toes. Tom didn't get hurt but he did, as he said, "learn to step lively."

Almost from the day he was born, Tom had sat on a horse's back. More than half a century later he was known worldwide as one of the greatest living horsemen. Could anyone have asked for a better life?

A painting of Belle Beach with Tom Bass up.

27

Grief

There was much to celebrate in Tom's professional life. Although a new generation of horse enthusiasts was replacing old horsemen like Tom, in 1927 the largest shows in the country paid tribute to him. The American Royal of Kansas City honored him as one of the event's founders. The Chicago horse show recognized Tom's great performance at the Columbian Exposition almost 35 years earlier. During the Madison Square Garden show, Tom was acclaimed as America's greatest individual horseman. The New York newspapers praised him, one calling him "An American Phenomenon."

The certificates and citations from these shows joined Tom's enormous collection of earlier honors. But what might have been a year of celebration turned to tragedy.

Tom's son had grown into a troubled young man.

He was an alcoholic and often sick. He would live at his parents' house for a few days and then leave, sometimes disappearing for weeks. Inman had found a job in Columbia, Missouri, but his drinking problems continued. In 1927, when he was only 30 years old, Inman died.

The lives of Angie and Tom came to a standstill. Family and friends helped make funeral arrangements. Many of the mourners who came to pay their respects were young men, Inman's age. They had either worked for Tom through the years or admired him from afar. Tom helped guide many of these young men and made a positive impact on their lives. Why hadn't he been able to do the same for his own son? Tom asked himself that question a thousand times, but there were no answers. There was only the grief. It pressed against him like a stampede of stallions.

Several days after Inman's funeral, Angie looked outside and saw Tom mounted on Belle Beach. The black coat of the 23-year-old mare glistened in the morning sunlight. Tom was dressed in his showman's black pants, coat, leather boots and bowler hat.

Tom's doctor had recently told him that his heart was weak. "You're headed for a heart attack, Tom," the doctor said, "if you don't stop riding."

The exertion could kill him – not to mention the dangers of a possible fall. But with the tragedy of

Inman's death, Tom felt a great longing to ride Belle Beach.

Tom saw Angie looking at him from the kitchen window. "A fine day for a dance on the square," he said.

When Tom and Belle Beach rode into Mexico, shopkeepers and customers came outside to see what was happening. Tom and the mare circled the square. Word quickly spread that Tom and Belle were in town. Hundreds of people began lining the sidewalks. Some climbed on top of wagons and cars for a better look. They cheered as Tom passed.

Tom and Belle performed for thirty minutes. They danced and whirled while the audience clapped and whistled. After making their final bow, Tom and Belle rode back to the barn, followed by a parade of fans. People who saw the show that day remembered it for years to come.

Later that night Tom told Angie that showing a horse in front of an audience was good medicine for an old man. For thirty minutes the medicine had helped him bear his grief.

Tom Bass and Belle Beach in retirement.

28

Goodbye to Champions

Tom knew the doctor was right. Performing was hard work and every year it seemed harder. In 1929 when Tom turned 70 years old, he decided to retire. He and Belle Beach would perform on the major circuit one last time. At 25 years old Belle Beach had won more trophies and ribbons than any mare in history.

It was another Tom Bass Year. From show to show – St. Louis, Chicago, Ottawa, Montreal, Denver, New York, Louisville, Los Angeles and Kansas City – Tom and Belle said their good byes. Mothers and fathers brought their children because they had seen Tom when they were young and didn't want their children to miss seeing the greatest living horseman. Many learned to ride at a Tom Bass Riding School. Event organizers scheduled Tom as the final performance – that way they knew the audience would stay for the whole show.

As her final act, Belle raised up on her back legs. Graceful as ever, the black mare extended her front hooves high overhead. And then in a new move, she let one front hoof droop down, as if she were waving good bye. Tom lifted his familiar bowler hat in a salute to his applauding fans. And then they were gone.

Back in Mexico, Tom tried to retire, but work had always been horses, the thing that gave meaning to his life. How could he retire from that?

With Angie's encouragement, Tom agreed to train a couple of horses.

"Nothing too strenuous," his doctor warned.

When his health stabilized in 1931, Tom decided to ride in the St. Louis Horse Show. He took a horse named Pearl, a little mare he'd recently trained.

Tom and Pearl rode in the five-gaited class. They were ahead of the competitors when Tom suddenly began to sway in the saddle. The audience watched in horror as he slumped forward over Pearl's neck.

Tom would not remember much of the incident. All he could recall was the crushing pain in his chest. Instinctively, his legs gripped the horse's sides. He had to be pried from the saddle.

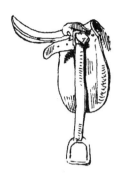 Tom survived the heart attack. Healing, however, was slow. A year later he tried to mount Pearl again, but he was so wobbly that even Tom knew his riding days were over. And so he began to plot ways he could train a horse without having to ride it. A bad heart might slow him physically, but it couldn't destroy his spirit.

One day he told Angie he was going to the barn. She watched him from the kitchen window, as she had a thousand times before. He was slower now, walking as if each step required concentration, but his tall body was still as erect as ever.

He hadn't been gone long when Angie heard the back door open. Tom slumped in a chair at the kitchen table.

"She's gone, Angie," he said. "Belle is dead."

Horses trained by him were performing all over the country. For years they would win ribbons and trophies. And for generations afterwards their sons and daughters would be champions. But none claimed Tom's heart like Belle Beach.

Tom's heart finally gave out, and on November 20, 1934, he died. Tributes to him ran in major newspapers in the United States, Canada and Europe. Everyone praised this remarkable man. Born into slavery, he achieved more than most people who had the advantages of money and position.

Tom Bass never set out to be the first black horseman to compete in a horse show. He never made it his goal to be the first black person to perform at Madison Square Garden or the St. Louis Horse Show or any of the other places where he broke racial barriers. And although it may have been a secret dream, he never set out to be a world champion horseman. And yet he achieved all these things.

Tom Bass loved and understood horses. He was, as his grandfather said, a natural. The rest followed.

Postscript

Tom Bass was laid to rest beside his son, Inman, in a segregated cemetery. In 1941, Angie was buried next to him. For many years his gravestone provided no indication of the remarkable man buried there.

In the late 1940s a group of Tom's friends and admirers began a campaign to erect a monument over his grave. Today a large marble stone, with Tom and Belle Beach carved on its surface, now marks the site.

In April 1999, Tom was inducted into the Hall of Famous Missourians. In honor of the horseman, 160 descendants and horse enthusiasts mounted horses and rode from Mexico, Missouri, to Jefferson City, the state's capital.

It is important that we honor Tom Bass in these ways. Historians have written about the racial barriers broken by famous sports people like Jackie Robinson, Jesse Owens and Althea Gibson. But long before these great athletes, there was Tom Bass. As long as we tell his story, Tom's hard-won contributions to the sport he loved will continue to inspire us to follow our own dreams.

Glossary

Aids: Legs, hands, weight and voice, as any of these are used to give commands to a horse.

Bit: The metal piece of the bridle that goes in the horse's mouth.

Bridle: The headgear worn by a horse and used to control the animal. It includes the headstall, bit and reins. Headstall is the part of the bridle that fits over the horse's head and attaches to the bit.

Broodmare: A mare used to produce foals.

Canter: A three-beat gait. Some people are reminded of a rocking horse when they see it.

Colt: A baby male horse under four years old.

Conformation: The shape or build of a horse. A horse with good conformation looks "balanced" and has a pleasing symmetry.

Filly: A baby female horse under four years old.

Foal: A colt or filly under one year old.

Gait: The movements of a horse. Three-gaited is the walk, trot and canter. Five-gaited is the walk, canter, trot and rack, plus a slow gait, such as running walk, fox trot or stepping pace.

Gelding: A male horse that has been made infertile.

Hand: A unit of measurement equal to four inches (10cm), about the width of a human hand. Horses are measured in hands, from the withers to the ground. American Saddlebred horses are from 15 hh to 16.1 hh.

Harness horse: An animal used for pulling a cart or carriage rather than for riding under saddle.

High School: A method of riding in which a horse performs to music, doing complicated and difficult movements. The routines of the Spanish Riding School in Vienna, Austria, provide good examples of this today.

Longe-line: a 20- to 30-foot rope used to train a horse by having the horse work in a circle around the trainer who is holding the line.

Mare: A mature female horse, four years or older.

Pedigree: A record of a horse's ancestry.

Points: The parts of a horse. (See page 29)

Rack: The fifth gait of the American Saddlebred. A fast and flashy, four-beat movement in which only one foot at a time touches the ground.

Saddle horse: A riding horse, one that is used "under saddle."

Stallion: A mature male horse that can be used for breeding.

Trot: A bouncy, two-beat gait in which one of the horse's back legs moves in unison with the front leg on the opposite side.

Walk: A slow movement in which the horse lifts each foot, one at a time.

J.L. Wilkerson, a native of Kentucky, now lives in Kansas City, Missouri. A former teacher, Wilkerson has worked as a writer and editor for more than 25 years. She is an award-winning writer whose essays and articles have appeared in professional journals and popular magazines in the United States and Great Britian. She is the author of several regional history books. Wilkerson also has written children's books, including other biographies for Acorn Books' The Great Heartlanders Series.

Information about Tom Bass's life and times and about horses is available through these resources:

Audrain County Historical Society, Mexico, Missouri.

Tom Bass: Black Horseman, by Bill Downey.

Kansas City, Missouri, Public Library, Special Collections.

American Royal Museum, Kansas City, Missouri.

The Illustrated Encyclopedia of Horse Breeds, by Susan McBane.

The Book of the Horse, by Samuel Sidney.

These and other sources were used during the research of *From Slave to World-Class Horseman: Tom Bass.*

ACORN BOOKS
THE GREAT HEARTLANDERS SERIES

Making history an active part of children's lives.

You can find this book and other Great Heartlanders books at your local fine bookstores.

For information about school rates for books and educational materials in THE GREAT HEARTLANDERS SERIES, contact

Acorn Books
THE GREAT HEARTLANDERS SERIES
7337 Terrace
Kansas City, MO 64114-1256

Other biographies in the series include:
Scribe of the Great Plains: Mari Sandoz
Champion of Arbor Day: J. Sterling Morton
A Doctor to Her People: Dr. Susan LaFlesche Picotte

Additional educational materials in THE GREAT HEARTLANDERS SERIES are

- ♦ Activities Books
- ♦ Maps
- ♦ Celebration Kits
- ♦ "Factoid" Bookmarks
- ♦ Posters

To receive a free Great Heartlanders catalog and a complete list of series books and educational materials, write or call Acorn Books.

Toll Free: 1-888-422-0320+READ (7323)
www.acornbks.com